MINDFUL MACHINES

NAVIGATING ETHICS AND VALUES

SUBHASH CHANDER THUKRAL

INDIA • SINGAPORE • MALAYSIA

ISBN 979-8-89133-428-1

Dedicated to

In honour of my wife

Late Smt. Neelam Kumari.

Table of Contents

Part 1

Ethics

CHAPTER - 1

Concept

Human by nature being a social animal, needs society to live, where one interacts with so many people of different ideologies, cultures and temperaments. Humans, being socialists, have a quality of getting maximum interaction with maximum people to get updated with the environment. It results in a lot of suggestions and ideas for the betterment of society and livelihood. It gets observed with the passage of time and also takes it necessary to analyze these suggestions and ideas on the basis of experiences and truth; it keeps us to the extract of suggestions by which it felt necessary that these suggestions be enforced and made acceptable to the society so that a disciplined environment may get established in the vicinity of the society for the betterment of livelihood. These suggestions were coordinated with the government and it was felt necessary that they be enforced on the public in the form of rules and regulations to streamline the living and control the violations. These rules and regulations form part of the ethics. Ethics at its simplest means morals and principles, which state what is good for humans, the environment and society. Second, we might have observed that all these have evolved from our daily routine activities; it took us to such thoughts where virtuous aspects prevailed and one felt happiness from the heart, so there is no hard way to implement it; rather, it encourages us to go in the right direction.

The world's oldest living civilization is in India (at present, it is in Afghanistan at the foothills of the Hindu Kush mountains).

It seems that in the heyday of Mohenjo-Daro and Harappa both big cities of the Indus Valley civilization, one of the world's greatest civilizations flourished on the land of Indus and Saraswati. Bharatvarsh (the Indian subcontinent) was home to the oldest civilization in the world. It then happens when people know the value of ethics. Indian ethics provides a basis for the holistic development of individuals, society and organizations. Philosophers had a great research work on ethics and presented to the world their best thoughts, that is, strengthening the law and haters of the false. The humans have accepted this very gracefully and consider ethics to be absolutely essential, not only for day-to-day activities but for the development of the nation too. Ethics accepts the law of right and earnestly seeks the truth. Ethics are primarily concerned with the moral issues of the world. People are required to discharge their duties according to the moral code of ethics. A true knowledge of ethics would be attained if one practiced and imbibed these moral laws. India has a very ancient history of knowledge about ethics. Its central concepts are represented in the Rig Vedas, one of the oldest knowledge texts. In the Rig Vedas, we come across the idea of all pervading cosmic order, which is denoted by *rta*. The term (*rta*) reflects in the Rig Vedas approximately four hundred and fifty times. It is a Vedic concept; it narrates the authority of God, so it pertains to all creatures of the universe; hence, it stands for harmony and balance in nature and human society. Here, *rta* is described as a power or force that is the controller of the forces of nature and of moral value in human society. In human society, when harmony and balance are destroyed, there is disorder and suffering. This is the power or force that lies behind nature and keeps everything in balance. It is the state of cosmic flow, which is dynamic and always progressing; moreover, what is natural is *RTA*. *RTA* (Sanskrit meaning: order, rule, truth) is the principle of natural order that regulates and coordinates the operation of the universe and everything within it. It is the (*rta*) that the sky and earth are firm, the sun rises, water flows, cows yield milk, constituted the ethical standard, which had a direct impact on the lives of the Vedic people and a harmony was maintained between nature and human's social lives. *RTA* in human spirituality is experiential spirituality; its experiential spirituality stands primarily on responsibility and morals based upon practical spiritual wisdom. *RTA* is not imaginary, philosophized or speculated; it is lived, performed, implemented, perceived and achieved. *RTA* is not evolved from prescription, forbidding order or absolute principles to be followed; it is simply the action in all realms of our life, reflecting the understanding of the spiritual meaning of responsibility in front of nature and human society. Understanding responsibility is not as simple an issue as the word reveals. The practical spiritual understanding of responsibility is for mankind, which is more real and important than the intellectual understanding of enlightenment; that is, whatever the Vedic religious or philosophical concept of oneness with God, the *RTA* is closer to the dignity of human life than to Atman. It is closer to the economy and social goodness than to religious obligation, it is closer to societal education than to religious norms and it is closer to responsibility than to any philosophical explanation of Dharma. Later it came to the word *SATYA*, that is, invariable truth, further it came to be widely known by the term Karma, which refer to both action and result of action. It works on certain universal principles, according to Vedas.

Ethics, a branch of moral philosophy, gives us a sense of rightness or wrongness and we act accordingly in the interest of society. It identifies good and bad, fair and unfair practices about moral duty. It is a set of rules that governs the person for right conduct and what should be an ideal human being. In the Vedas, ethics is considered a moral duty of the doer toward the material world, which makes the human being purer and clearer from the inner senses and puts them into rational thinking. The Vedas assert that the divine law is the standard of morals and good conduct, which makes us enthusiastic for spiritualism, socialism and patriotism.

It is observed that the Almighty not only created the universe but also made the creation purposeful by putting the human being on a pendulum through the divine knowledge of the Vedas. The knowledge of the Vedas teaches us the way of living in the sense of right and wrong and it is the human being who has to decide through his mind which is to be adopted for a purposeful life. The ethical ideals emanate with all their purposefulness from the divine nature of the self to social evolution. Ethics makes a human being a visionary, a vision of reality means true in all aspects, a reality that gives satisfaction to the human being and humanity. The world has accepted this, followed the ethics and put their theories pertaining to the ethics accordingly.

CHAPTER - 2

Evolution

Greek Philosophy: Socrates, a great teacher in the field of ethics, observed that "the unexamined life is not worth living". Plato, the student of Socrates, stressed the happiness of life, which comes from wisdom in human beings. Wisdom is considered the highest human goodness. The goodness is that any action that, satisfies all good, it is the opposite of evil which is misfortune for society. Everybody wants to keep away from such acts because evil is such an act that makes everyone unhappy. Aristotle, a Greek philosopher, termed virtue the highest ethical value and considered that when a person acts in accordance with virtue it is observed that person feels himself satisfied and contented. The philosopher asserted that "nature does nothing in vain", a person interacting with nature and meeting their desires from nature without any ecological disturbance is understood as a real virtue. The knowledge of the self is essential for personal growth, decision-making and accurate self-assessment understanding the difference between good and bad—leads one to happiness. It is wisdom and research that frees one from all evils. So, everything is good when there is a check on every action and that check is the study of ethics.

Socrates and Plato are regarded as the fathers of Western philosophy, following in the footsteps of Greek philosophers. The philosophy has been classified into three categories. The first, Western hold of the Aristotelian work, Aristotle, holds that the virtues (such as justice, charity and generosity) are positions to act in such a way that the person and the person's society both get benefits. The second is that humans are bound to do their duty with sincerity and dedication so having knowledge of their duty makes the environment rational and ensures the best results. Thirdly, utilitarianism means the action that gives happiness or benefit to the greatest number.

Indian philosophy**:** The study of Indian ethical thoughts in writing begins with the origin of the Rig Veda, the oldest scripture in the world. This means that ethics in India are from a very past time when there was oral tradition to pass the communiqué and most of the world was living life like nomads. This reflects India's identity which was so rich in civilization, social organization and intellectual outlook that it can be well recognized and understood by our existing old monuments, which show that the purpose of any construction is for a specific cause and their utility, it may be viewed in the service of mankind. Secondly, India being known as the center for spirituality means a disciplined state as our history reveals. So, it keeps us in mind that the Indian philosophers (*Rishis*) did great research on ethics and made it mandatory to follow a disciplinary life that is "a happy life", a life that gives happiness to others. Ethics in the Indian context is a composite intersection of spirituality, philosophy and morality.

Spirituality stresses that to live as a human being and how to acquire humanism must be the aim of life; to make it possible, it is mandatory to follow these versions.

Service and sacrifice: a universal version, Service to humanity is service to God; it means any action of a human should be sincere and corruption-free, as any action is our Karma, which is devoted to God; this is the highest service. Sacrifice was originally a gift from God to maintain harmony in the environment. Similarly, a human being is also God's image with a firm belief that a human being has a soul within him reflecting God's real being, as per old scripture (Vedas). So, to sacrifice for a human being in the form of material, time and place is a great virtue which means it is devotion to God.

Forgiveness, non-anger: "To err is human, to forgive is divine", a universal truth. Forgiveness is a gift to us; it is a quality that recognizes humans as the best human beings. To forgive others means to protect humanity in spite of others having harmed us; forgiveness is the supreme peace.

Non-anger, anger is a basic human emotion experienced by all pre-experiences when something has gone wrong in our environment. It is badly treated as excessive anger puts one mentally ill, raises blood pressure and ultimately leads to fatality. Though its motive is to find the solution to one's problem, it has been observed that whether it gets the problem solved or not it makes one feel ill, so we assert that ultimately there should be no anger which leads us to a peaceful life.

In Indian philosophy ethics is a conscious living within the certain rules laid down in the old scriptures, considering these an authority and making a distinction between "what is" and "what ought to be." The government has also authenticated these scriptures and made them laws to enforce on the public to maintain peace and harmony in society. These ethical beliefs explore the question of how we should live, what Aristotle called "a life well lived" and what defines us as human beings. Ethics makes us capable of answering these questions and providing reasons for our beliefs. "Is ethics descriptive?" means what is the history of ethics? Ethics starts with the existence of humans on this planet, as humans have brains to keep the difference between good and evil and its inscription is available in the Rig Vedas at least seven thousand years ago. After that, the origin of Western philosophy evolved, which is being practiced to date. The philosophy generally follows the Greek philosophy, whereas "ought" ethics is prescriptive, based on moral principles and behavior and defines what is right, good and proper. Real ethics, or ought ethics, is not concerned with the way things are but with the way they ought to be. It is considered that the person using ethics must be honest and dependable. Next comes, "How should we live?" It is asserted that every human being needs "A happy life". One feels happiness when one's life is being fulfilled by one's needs; that is, it is satisfaction that makes one do so. The question is, how does one feel satisfied? It is when we fulfill the needs of others without any desires, then, we feel happy. Secondly, contentment is happiness, a universal truth; contentment means the basic needs or the quality of life of a human being, which one considers a suffice in socially, politically and economically; we call it a contented life. What is the need of a human being? As per scientific studies and research work on happiness theories, human needs are identified as:

i. **Well-being**. our body should be well versed by the mind and must have all physical interactions; that is, one must be free from diseases.

ii. **Environment**. A clean and safe environment to live in is a necessity for a happy life.

iii. **Relationship**. Human beings, being social animals, need a good society for interactions; involvement in social activity gives one's heartfelt satisfaction.

iv. **Success is peace of mind**; one gets self-satisfied knowing that his accomplishment has value.

v. **Elasticity**. Negative events do come into our lives; a safe outcome from such events leads us to a happy life.

vi. **Contentment**. To understand the meaning of contentment is to have real wisdom. Contentment is a state of mind that brings happiness and quality to life, where money is not a criterion.

Indian philosophy holds the belief that our present circumstances are a result of our past actions, deeply ingrained in our nature. Therefore, one should find contentment in what one has. Furthermore, the inherent conscience within the human body guides individuals to distinguish between right and wrong, taking into account the consequences of their actions. People seek the path of righteousness and truthfulness to lead a happy life, as per the teachings of our ancient scriptures. Following these principles is the only way to secure both one's present and future.

Bookish knowledge prioritizes one's happiness and leads one to follow the materialistic world, which is momentarily pleasure and satisfaction for a short time; it does not last long and puts one in distress; one must remain far away from such activities. The Vedic books are the only ones that encourage one to move toward spiritual knowledge, which explains the difference between "need" and "desire" and helps one understand that one must feel satisfied with the completion of needs, not the completion of desires. Desire is an attitude aimed at something believed to be good. Desire is a continuous process that never ends. Philosophy names this as a life force but also calls it the great symbol of sin, as desire is, of course, called greed and greed is insatiable. So, contentment gives you satisfaction; it does not disallow one to stop striving for a better one, but to be satisfied with the results of our efforts. The Vedic philosophy views ethics as the study of the nature of the cosmos and the study of humanity. The study of the cosmos is the study of a natural science, considering the universe as a whole with its object as a physical entity and a composition of matter, energy and its inter-relationships (pertaining to the natural science). The theory is based on reason. On the other hand, the world's scholars also put forth their views, considering the universe as the natural context of a living being; that is, we can experience the universe through our participation in and the response of humanity to that of nature (pertaining to human science); the evidence is based on experience. In this way, we come to the conclusion that humans are a part of this universe, as humans are also a composition of matter and energy. In this way, every activity in the universe affects the nature of humanity. So, to understand the universe, a joint effort between astronomy and physics is essential. Astronomy is the study of the objects above the earth's atmosphere; an amazing thing is that every object remains moving all the time and it is gravity that holds all this, whereas physics is the natural science that studies matter and energy. Therefore, to understand the nature of cosmology, physics and astrophysics (the branch of astronomy) play a vital role in understanding the universe through scientific observations and experiments. Natural science may be more reliable as it is taken into consideration that every happening in this universe is due to some reasons, the results of which one compares with one's physical life and which proved to be as it affects the physique of the human.

The study of human science is based on time-to-time experience, whereas the study of the nature of the cosmos is based on relevant facts and ideas. It is asserted that both sciences are related to each other and are capable of supporting each other. Cosmology is the scientific study of the universe's origin and evolution. Modern cosmic science, whose birth is not more than two hundred years ago, is putting forth its best efforts to study the nature of the cosmos, but it is so nature-bound that its script is well inscribed in Vedic texts, which one can access to move ahead. The science that claimed to be the apex agency reached a fraction of this system and came to the result that there is some power (*God*) that has created this supreme and formless being; the reason behind this creation is unknown. Modern science has come to the conclusion that following the Vedic text, which the Indian scientists (*Rishis*) wrote thousands of years ago, possesses great knowledge to understand the nature of cosmology. As per the Vedic text, all the objects of the universe existed in a subtle form inside God and when God desired it, it was manifested as it is in the present form, controlled by God. There is no beginning or end and it is understood to be infinite and cyclic. The Vedic literature came into existence long before the development of modern science, but with the passage of time, societies shifted their thinking from the Vedas to a materialistic world, which is due to humans' nature for instantaneous results, that is, the use of inorganic sciences for living. Every entity has a fixed time to develop, but it can be done instantaneously by inorganic processing, which is violating nature, that is, living in a hazardous life, which may be avoided. In this way, the Vedas get absolute but this has not to run so long as "who runs fast that ends early" a universal truth. The world's scientists have acknowledged the Vedas, the text from which we have the treasure of knowledge. The five great elements of nature, "Earth, Water, Air, Fire and Sky," by virtue of which the existence of life gets possible and the combination of all these forms a universe and as per our old scripture, it is the first and foremost duty of the human being to save the universe by not creating any such polluting activity that may prove to be a deterioration factor for nature. The whole universe is created by matter and matter is a composition of electrons and protons and the unification of these creates the basis of molecular theory. In modern molecular theory, the proton of positive charge resides in the nucleus and the electron of negative charge revolves around the proton of the atom. In this context, this definition is somewhat similar to the Vedic literature. In Vedic literature, "Yaju" derives from two words, "Yat" and "Ju." "Yat" denotes constantly moving and "Ju" denotes stationary, indicating that the combination of these two elements is at the core of everything. It is a clear interpretation that the electron and proton of modern molecular theory have replaced "*Yaju*" and "Ju" in Vedic scientific literature. In the Vedas "*Yaju*" and "Ju" have been named "Vaju" and "Akash". Cosmology is a branch of astronomy that involves the origin and evolution of the universe. According to NASA, the definition of cosmology is the "scientific study of the large-scale properties of the universe as a whole." Another definition of cosmology, it is "the branch of philosophy dealing with the general structure of the universe, with its parts, elements and laws and especially with such of its characteristics as space, time, causality and freedom." The objective of the Vedic studies is, first, to reveal the scientific description of the cosmos to mankind. Second, to discuss the relevance of the incomparable knowledge of the Veda, which is as latest as it is. Thirdly, Sanskrit literature is a great carrier of Indian heritage and every Indian should know about this.

vii. **Morality**. Means "character, proper behavior." Character means the quality or features of a human being that make up their identity. Behavior, the behavior of human beings, is generally counted by external stimuli, as the well-behaved person sometimes becomes very furious, so it reflects that human beings behave as per the prevailing situation of the environment; if the environment is peaceful and enjoyable, this gives a soothing relief to human beings; one's is automatically a sense of good behavior; if the environment is noisy and furious, then the behavior of the one's becomes bad, that is, as per the prevailing environment. Ultimately, human beings should have good behavior whether the environment is joyful or sorrowful. Both are part of life; these are inevitable so humans must behave in a nice way in any situation. The behavior of a human being should please everyone, as it also reflects the identity of the human being. The duties of humanity are controlled by morality, as morality is the necessary condition to live a good life. Morality is an understanding of right and wrong under the supervision of the conscience. Morality mainly comes from three sources:

a. **Genes**. Genes are the first source of our morality; it is said that heredity flows in the human being. If we go to the past, right from the very beginning, when everyone was good and to live a morally able life was the aim of life, the teachings of our old scripture were morally so strong and distinguished that there was no room for an immoral entity. As history reveals, there exists good and evil and one cannot escape from this. Good and evil are relative terms; good cannot exist without evil and evil exists only in relation to good. So, one has to face both, but it is asserted that our ancestors followed more goods as their lives were very peaceful, with the same result passing on to us. We accordingly follow that, realizing the difference between good and evil and come to the conclusion that to live a peaceful and dignified life, one has to adopt a morally sound life.

b. **Societies**. A man is known by the society in which he lives. Aristotle said a long time ago that a human being is a social animal because sociality is in his natural instinct; one cannot live without society. The human being is a composition of matter and energy and matter is a natural entity. Our oldest scripture puts stress on worshiping nature. Our existence is due to the existence of nature. Nature has influenced our body and our system of living by providing us with fresh air and pure water, which are the ultimate sources of life on this planet. Without nature, we are no more. It becomes clear from this version that man has a natural instinct in him. Society is an organization of like-minded people where people of different sorts gather on one platform to exchange their views for the betterment of their livelihood. Life is so complex today that one needs society to maintain relations, that is, social relations, professional relations and so on. In essence, society is a way of life; it is a group of people where we have likeness and differences, we have cooperation and conflicts and even though it is abstract we realize the society; we can't touch or see it. It has many functions that help to run an ideal life and common objectives to develop the whole society in all aspects. In a society where one has the opportunity to interact with so many people, the culture of the society has ups and downs in the conversations but in spite of all these it puts the individuals to keep a moral life. In this way society has a role in setting the morality of the individual; it keeps the environment rational and a demand of the day.

c. **Professions**. A profession is an occupation that a human being has to undertake to maintain his family and society. Every profession is bound by certain rules and regulations, which leads to a workable and comfortable environment. A professional has to spend more than eight hours a day in his organization to achieve the accomplishment; that is, a human being has to spend 33% of his working lifetime with the organization with which one is associated. So, the human being learns a lot in this environment; thereby, one gets to interact with different kinds of people with different kinds of knowledge. In spite of all these, the organization has only one goal, which is to grow, to follow universal truth, which is only possible by adopting the culture of fairness and right approach in every action. This is the first and basic principle of a growing organization.

A human being who is at his or her workable, societal and learnable age grasps everything very easily and acts accordingly. In this materialistic world, where good and bad both exist it is now up to him to decide, what is the best for him. It is obvious that everyone always chooses "the best", the good, though the bad exists here as more shining; moreover, the culture of the organization is committed to chosen growth, which is possible by choosing the good practices, whereas one has committed to follow the good. In this way the profession of a human being plays a great role in setting the morality of a human being.

We as human beings have to follow these to live a happy life and to be an ideal for others so that everyone lives a happy life, to live life with ethical values. The world's oldest literary text full of whole universe knowledge, the Vedas, A brief description of the Vedas:

The Rig Veda is presumed to be the oldest text, compiled by Rishi Vyas. It is the principle of all Vedas, as it has detailed literature on the social, spiritual, political and economic background of the Vedic civilization. Rig Veda has knowledge of cosmology and tallying with modern science. The concept of Rta comes from the Rig Veda, which means cosmic and sacred order, an ultimate and harmonically integrated structure of reality. Rite and right both are versions of Rta. It is a composition of 1028 hymns (*Suktas*) and 10600 verses in all, organized into ten different mandalas (the books). The hymns predominantly discuss cosmology.

Yajurveda: The Yajurveda has knowledge of the performance of rituals and ceremonies. "Yajur" is derived from the Sanskrit word "yajus," which means worship or sacrifice and "Veda" means knowledge. Therefore, Yajurveda is the knowledge of sacrifice.

It is believed to have been composed between 1200 and 900 BCE. The Yajur Veda is divided into two parts: the white or pure Yajurveda, known as Shukla and the dark or black Yajurveda, known as Krishna. The white or pure Yajurveda consists of prayers and specific instructions for devotional sacrifices, while the black Yajur Veda deals with sacrificial rituals. Adhvaryu was the expert in the knowledge of the Yajurveda.

Sama Veda: Sama Veda sets hymns from the Rig Veda to music, to be chanted at appropriate stages with proper notes. It is often called the Veda of melodies and chants and is divided into two major parts. The first part includes the four melody collections or the Saman, which are the songs and the latter part is the Arcika, or the verse books, which are a collection of (Samhita) hymns. Sama Veda has 1875 verses, out of which seventy-five verses are from the Rig Veda. Our classical music has its roots in this Veda. If Rig Veda is the word, Sama Veda is the song or meaning. Sama Veda comprises a number of texts dealing with various subjects. Its primary purpose is liturgical. It is believed to have been composed around 1200 to 1000 BCE.

Atharva Veda: The Atharva Veda has knowledge of Ayurveda, the science of health and longevity, as well as ethical principles. The Veda is described as a "knowledge storehouse of Atharvanas," which means formulas and spells intended to counteract diseases and calamities, or "the procedure for everyday life." This scripture has its own identity and also contains knowledge of some distinct rituals. It is composed in Vedic Sanskrit and is a collection of 730 hymns with about 6000 mantras divided into 20 books. It is believed that the Atharva Veda was composed during the 2nd millennium BCE.

The Vedas are the earliest texts to have recognized ethics as the most basic element in human life. Ethics have a divine origin; one simply has to adopt it. Ethics, or moral philosophy, is a branch of philosophy based on the basic principles of truth and honesty. Truth is the law of the universe; 'God is the source of truth." Speak truthfully and act truthfully; it assures that God escorts us on to the path of righteousness. (Rig Veda. V.82.7). Sins are those that displease anyone, even disorder to the environment means displeasing God, disturbing ecology system by emission of more carbon gases by men for petty self-interests that is to earn more or to show super technocracy are also sins, while acts of charity, helping others, truthfulness, self-control, chastity, courage and humility are considered virtues. This led us on to the path of righteousness, which must be the ultimate aim of life. The Vedas, the oldest and most complete knowledge text on our planet today, originates from the ancient Indian subcontinent (presently Pakistan and North West India), when there was no caste or creed and only humanity prevailed. Vedas come into existence in Sanskrit. Vedas means to know, leading to Vidya (knowledge). The Vedas are the books of changeless reality. As history reveals, we do not know the author of these texts. The Vedas came to us in Vedic Sanskrit written form about 4000-6000 years ago. It is supposed that this knowledge was transmitted orally over many generations to keep the knowledge alive before eventually being committed to writing. It is said that it was skillfully created by Rishis (*sages*) in India. These text books cover the complete knowledge of the material world as well as the spiritual world, which has influenced the scholars of the world. So, the Vedas are considered to have a divine origin and are also called Sruti (what is heard) literature. Therefore, these texts are not of any religion, but they are for all and exceptionally applicable to all. The Vedas are universally accepted as they have the knowledge of the eternal, the knowledge of mankind and the knowledge of the self.

CHAPTER - 3

Aspects

Knowledge of the eternal: eternal means "everlasting," but when we speak in context to the universe, it means eternal truth. Eternal truth is an entity or a proposition that is true with no relation to time; that is, it is true not only always but always with absolute necessity. Words are of two types: eternal and effectual. The words that represent relation with specific perfect knowledge, that is, all rivers of the universe flow into one ocean without ever filling it, the unalterable course of the sun from day-to-day and the succession of day and night are examples of eternal. The words created by us are functions of various factors, such as our existing knowledge, tendencies and events; that is, these words have their effects up to certain limits and are therefore not eternal. Just as God is eternal, so is his knowledge. The Vedas, which we believe to be God's knowledge, represent eternal knowledge, the knowledge that has no author, is neither increased or decreased nor variable and has existence throughout time, just as creation is infinite and eternal, without beginning and without end. So, is the Vedic knowledge? It is an ongoing process; no one knows its starts and no one knows its ends; it is eternal. The Veda states that God created the universe as, as it was created previously, the same text as it is now, the same eternal knowledge of the Vedas. Hence, Vedas, knowledge is believed to be eternal knowledge. This knowledge in India is then, when the rest of the world is in feeble condition and the hard work of our Rishis makes it possible to discover the truth of the eternal. This gives the nation the vision of eternity in all things and the feeling of the presence of God in themselves and in all around them. Rishis asserted that truth is not only for morality nor for the sake of society, but a preparation and purification of the soul by which human beings become capable of coming out of the dark pit of bodily, mental and emotional selfishness into the clear heaven of love and benevolence and puts the individual in a state where one can align himself with the supreme God, which must be the ultimate aim of life. The source of knowledge is our education system, which from generation to generation facilitates the universe in transmitting knowledge to make its best use for society. The truths are eternal and their study reveals that "God is truth" that always exists and that its events such as air, water, earth, fire and sky stay fixed. Some thinkers assert that the knowledge gained by the organs remains in continuous flow, which makes one capable of recollecting the past. The existence of this continuous knowledge shows the development and understanding of knowledge in the mind of the individual. This eternal knowledge is with the soul from the time of birth up to the time of death and destruction of it never occurs. These are the wonders of God. It is education that helps reduce poverty and fulfill the dreams of aspirants. The core message of Vedic scripture is "freedom," which is applicable in all aspects and the Vedic scientist, whom we call "Rishi," realized this knowledge of eternal truth and developed methods by meditating on the inner self of a human being and putting them into the universe, which proved to be reliable and can be put into practice, considers it to be the most rigorous scientific study. The Rishis developed technologies like Yoga and meditation, by which not only physical and mental well-being can be achieved but also the cosmic mystery of "consciousness" can be realized. The Vedas are the most ancient scriptures in the world. The eternal laws of life and the universe expressed in these scriptures were revealed by Rishis, who devoted their entire lives to the realization of the ultimate truth. This knowledge they received not through a sense of perception or the mind but through an inner vision from the source of the soul during the deepest states of contemplation and meditation. There are seven universal laws that govern this entire universe and keep everything in perfect harmony. The first three are immutable, that is, eternal, which means absolute and not changeable and the next four are mutable, that is, transitory, which means the laws can be used to create better our own realities.

The law of mentalism, states that all is the mind, the universe is also a mental entity, it means that the mind or consciousness is the basic things of the entire universe and the consciousness is the mind of the absolute universal mind. It holds true on all planes, that is, the physical, the mental and the spiritual. 'All is the mind' does not mean that every activity belongs to the mental plane, but the mental plane is that plane that we consider to be mental activities such as thinking, imagination and our overall mental state. Our mind is one and the same as the universal mind in its entirety. Our reality is the concept of our mind, that is, an image of our consciousness since all is mind. It means we do not have a mind, but we are the mind; it is the essence of mind power.

The law of correspondence, also known as the law of analogy, states that "as above so below, as below so above, as within so without, as without so within, it means there exists harmony, agreement and correspondence between the physical, mental and spiritual planes; it means our outer world is the reflection of our inner world and keeps us well identified with what is currently going on inside of us. Our philosopher narrated it as: "Change the way we look at things and the things we look at change". It means when we are aligned within, the world around us will align perfectly, too.

The law of vibration states that the whole universe is constantly moving or vibrating, which means everything has energy. It is stated that whatever we put into the universe through our thoughts, our actions, exactly it will come back to us. Albert Einstein put it most briefly and said, "Everything is energy. Match the frequency of the reality that we want and we cannot help but get that reality. This is not philosophy; this is physics. Match the energy that we wish for and it is ours.

The Law of Polarity states that everything that exists in this universe has an opposite; that is, everything is dual; everything has poles; everything has opposites. It means that the things that appear to be opposite are actually two extremes of the same thing, such as light and dark, hot and cold and so on. Many of us are living in this duality consciousness, swinging at the extreme, feeling unrest in our lives. However, this duality only exists in the physical and mental realms, whereas it does not exist in the spiritual realm, where everything is one. We can transform our realities from hate to love, dark to light and so on, by consciously raising our vibrations. Which is known as the ancient hermetic teaching of the Art of Polarization.

The Law of Rhythm states that everything has a rhythm. For example, we observe that wherever the sun shines, sometimes later we observe shadows there, which means everything flows positively as well as negatively. It means the universe also flows in rhythm; that is, we must be aware of rhythm because it may not get us down. There are ups and downs in life. If we feel that we are moving down, we should not worry; the swing will definitely come up, provided our thoughts are rational, which keeps us stronger and increases our enthusiasm to face the downfall.

The Law of Cause and Effect states that every cause has effects and every effect is due to a certain cause, which means our thoughts or actions transmitted from us have certain effects whether they are desirable or not. The law is applicable on all three planes, that is, physical, mental and spiritual. In the spiritual plane the effects are instantaneous whereas in the physical and mental planes, the effects of our thoughts materialize at different times. It is observed that whatever thoughts we think to conserve, they get converted into our reality. The more we focus on a certain entity, the more likely it is that it happened in our lives. So, we come to the conclusion that our future depends upon our way of thinking. If we go on negative thinking our lives will get negative results. So, as a conscious one, one gets the place where one places one's focus.

According to the Law of Gender, we must keep in mind that gender is in everything; that is, everything has its masculine and feminine qualities. It happened on all planes; creation is not possible without this law. The path to success is that when we understand the masculine and feminine principles, it leads us to maintain balance between the two and makes us fully aware of the physical, social and spiritual context. We are co-creators with the universe, so it becomes our duty to be aware of our thoughts, intentions, actions and ultimately our inner state. It gives us an opportunity to maintain balance in our hearts, minds, bodies and souls. The knowledge that we receive in schools and universities leads us to the material world, that is, a job, money and prestige. But this knowledge does not transform us into spiritualists and we remain the same with our uncertainties and our weaknesses. Meditation or esoteric knowledge, on the other hand, may not give us position or prestige but transform us in doing so, that is, our duty; it leads our approach to the divine world and gives us the meaning of life and eternity. If God has always been the same, the God will always bless us with his eternal knowledge, that is, the knowledge of the Vedas. It is observed that experiences give rise to good habits; good habits give rise to memory and we use this memory to decide what to accept and what to reject. In the absence of the habit of studying, even memory loss comes into existence, resulting in the halt of knowledge growth. Thus, it does not happen unless God did not kickstart this process at the inception of civilization; this process of pursuit of knowledge would not have started at all, just as it did not start in the animal world. The Vedas are regarded as revelations of eternal truths, to which no human season could ever challenge, which is due to the naturally developed reason of confidence and still lacks in its ability to unravel the mysteries of human beings and of the universe. The Vedas are nothing but a body of commands and prohibitions to make the human being an ideal for others.

Knowledge of mankind: Any action is called Karma, the result of which reflects our identity in every aspect; every action has good aspects as well as bad aspects; good aspects are liked by everyone and pleased by everyone; so, actions proved to be good are called mankind. Mankind, in turn, carries a special responsibility to lift the underlying people to equality with privileged people and to develop a sense of well-being because it is believed that mankind and spirituality move side by side, that is, both have an impression of goodness on the life of humans; it is well evolved for universal kinship and being of humans; it is a life high in welfare. Mankind has the capability to embrace the reality of diversity and relish in human freedom through its philosophy of pluralism, It means, that though we have varying likes and dislikes, our different cultures, not only do we get united to each other under the pretext of mankind in our own unique ways, but we also get a sense of wisdom, which keeps us duty-bound both socially and spiritually. The knowledge contained in the Vedas is for all mankind without any distinction. It has a universal appeal and purpose, which is clearly stated in one of the Vedic verses, quoted as “Let all men meet and think with one mind.

Let all hearts unite in love. Let God be common to all. May all live in happiness with a common purpose". The Vedas asserted that it is mankind that has common ideals and objectives: to live in harmony, to have common aspirations, to work for mutual cooperation, to have love and respect for society and to work for its progress. The Vedas uphold the equality of mankind. "All men are equal in brotherhood; there is no one small and no one big marching forward to prosperity." The teachings of the Vedas represent the original knowledge believed to have been given by God to mankind. It is the duty of mankind to study, understand and develop this knowledge for individual and universal welfare. The main purpose of this divine knowledge contained in the Vedas is to guide human beings to live a meaningful, progressive, happy and righteous life in the material world and also to plan for the future and final goal of life. The Vedas represent perfect harmony between matter and spirit, without any negative attitudes that lead to disillusion or ignorance. It indicates and projects a positive approach toward the acceptance of life in its fullness, the reality of death and life's struggles, deficiencies and imperfections. The Vedas point toward the ultimate reality, the eternal law and values based on morality and righteousness. The Vedas are full of divine wisdom. It is asserted that all useful knowledge for the good of humanity flows from the eternal fountain spring of the Vedas. It is therefore asserted that the Vedas contain the essence of all sciences in seed form, which we have to recover, extend and make applicable in practical life for the welfare of mankind. Vedas, which contain divine knowledge, have made it mandatory for all human beings to live life in accordance with their instructions. Mankind is believed to have the right to happiness, which is considered to be the most fundamental right of all humans. Mankind makes us well-equipped to live in this materialistic and spiritual world. To make it possible we must have three qualities. The mode of goodness, passion and ignorance

The mode of goodness is the sinless and supreme one, being purer than the other, being liked by everyone, being illuminating and freeing oneself from all sinful activities, making a sense of happiness and knowledge. The mode of passion in humans is a desirous one and these desires act as fuel for passion, which brings the greatest results in one's life. Its synonymous is determination, which puts one by heart to achieve goodness. In the mode of ignorance, a person's lack of knowledge means less education, being unaware of the state and knowing less about socialism, which leads to darkness and delusion about all embodied living entities. It is believed that all three qualities of nature at different levels live in human beings and we have control over them.

Above these modes, there are also unlimited opportunities created by nature which, through the combination of these modes of nature and opportunities, under the control and purview of eternal time, lead us to activities known as Karma. Karma deals with the pursuit of pleasure in the material world. It is believed that a human being's enjoyment or suffering is the result of their own deeds and actions committed in their previous life and in the present life. According to our ancient scriptures, there are four types of Karma: *Sanchita* or stored Karma is the accumulation of present and past fruits of our actions. In this type of Karma, our good actions cannot cancel out our bad actions; they coexist. The joy and sorrow in our lives are the outcomes of these actions. *Prarabdha* Karma or matured Karma is like an arrow released from a bow and is about to reach its destination. It can be likened to words spoken from our mouths, which cannot be taken back. It is a part of Sanchita Karma and is also referred to as predestination Karma.

Kriyamana Karma or present Karma is the fruit of our present actions.

Agami Karma is a part of Prarabdha Karma and can be thought of as the arrow that has been released and, if circumstances permit, will reach its destination. In other words, the choices we make today have a direct bearing on our future tomorrow. It is a mandatory Karma and we must make decisions about the events we seek.

Karma reminds us that there are consequences to all our actions, whatever a human being sows, a human being has to reap. Bhagavad Gita has delivered the lesson of mankind from the nuisance of material existence to the purpose of our existence. Every one of us is full of anxieties because of this material existence which we must avoid as much as we can as it makes us corrupt to fulfill the desires of this material world, which is the only cause of our anxieties. Our very existence is in the atmosphere of non- existence and there is no threat to human life by this non- existence. Our existence is eternal. But somehow or other we have been put into "ASAT" which refers to that which does not exist; it develops anxiety, which we find presently common in people. The Gita transcends the divine wisdom addressed to mankind at all times in order to help human beings. Mankind enrolls us as an ideal for others, considering its subjectivity and objectivity.

Subjectivity and Objectivity. Human being, a unique one, has beliefs and principles. Our thinking may vary from person to person but we are similar in certain things such as not to murder, not to steal, not to lie and so on, as this has come from our ancestors from where our ancestors got all these. Our ancestors got all these from our oldest scripture, the Vedas, which we consider to have divine knowledge. The whole universe has accepted this knowledge and has followed its norms and principles. The Vedas asserted the definition of right and wrong; the same was implemented by our ancestors and accordingly, it comes to us. Mankind, in the simplest terms, is the belief that mankind is universal and its every act is for the universal welfare, so it is not up for interpretation. Humans are at the top of all creations but they need a society to live in one cannot live alone and it is also a fact that humans have feelings and emotions, which put us to perform actions and affect the thinking of others too, which gives us an identity in the society. As such, one builds relationships with others in society and in the world over. One has family, friends and associates with good and bad company and becomes a unit of the family, society, country and world as a whole. In order to maintain this, one has to build good morals and socially adaptable qualities, which can only be possible when our actions prove to be for right thinking, which leads us to peaceful living. This is mankind and it is objective when we have a common object, that is, to work for a happy society. Objective sticks to the facts, whereas subjective is influenced by or based on personal beliefs or feelings rather than based on facts. The common purpose is objective and the personal purpose is subjective. A happy society exists when there is peace and the peace prevails when everybody performs their duties with discipline and discipline exists when people are ethical. Everybody wants peace and prosperity; it means a happy life; it constitutes a happy society, so working for a happy society is an objective and it has proved to be true for people of all cultures and at all times. On the other hand, the other thinker thinks that a society that paces with time and is well-equipped with modern infrastructure is considered to be a happy society, whereas it is observed that it results in the erosion of ethics and indulging in bad habits. Such scenarios may erode our culture and beliefs; this is subjectivity, which means it is true for the person(s) making the judgment of such scenarios even though it may not be true for others. Since objectivity does not guarantee truth and subjectivity is not necessarily false, it makes sense that objectivity is not the opposite of subjectivity. Subjectivity and objectivity have their own meanings and values. The term objective in philosophy refers to the idea that there are universal moral laws like good and bad, right and wrong and therefore these morals exist outside of any person, that is, the moral law that exists independently of any person. Mankind is a set of universal norms that aspires to reach the destination in a discipline, that is, perceived as best. Mankind is the only one to be grasped in the context of humans and humanity, which is understood as the best art to live a dignified life. We care about stuff, about our own well-being, about those who love us, about our tribe and it is mankind that has the capability of a sense of reciprocity and justice. Our devotion to God, as manifested by our actions, has had a profound impact on the spirit of mankind. The Gita is the most systematic statement of spiritual evolution, endowing value to mankind. Human beings are designed in such a way that eating is necessary the reason to go to work every day. This helps to keep one's physical fitness up and out of trouble. God is wise. A life is good if it performs its function well and is said to have "virtue". So, in Aristotelian terms, knowing the purpose of mankind or of human beings amounts to what are the human virtues and vices and this is a very large part of the aim of Aristotle's ethics: to tell us what counts as human virtue and what is good for mankind. Knowing what to count as human virtue pretty much fills the detailed account of human purpose.

Truth itself is the highest virtue; according to the Vedas, all virtues become vice without truth. There is no virtue nobler than truth. A noble human being should embody the following virtues: Always speak the truth. Anger must be avoided. Be a forgiver. There is only one legitimate wife. Wealth, whose lust creates indiscipline in nature must be taken into consideration in the distribution of wealth. Be simple. Don't harm anyone. Support the needy.

Knowledge of the Self. Self-knowledge, is the highest level of knowledge; this knowledge is related to the self, related to God and which is an eternal truth. If we are well aware of the knowledge of truth, it is known as philosophy and the person who knows the knowledge of truth is known as a philosopher. If we experience this knowledge of truth, this is known as mysticism and the people who experience this knowledge are known as mystics. It is very strange to say that the Almighty constituted the anatomy of all humans the same, but we are all different in aspects of knowledge, which is not simply important but the only component that makes us capable of running a valuable life. So, it becomes interesting that we must study this knowledge. It is observed that humans feel themselves enclosed in three states: the physical world, the social world and the psychological world of thoughts, feelings and behavior and it becomes the duty of humans to know about all these as they may prove useful for one's life.

The physical world endorses for us the length, breadth and environment of the universe, which enables us to determine the living condition of humans in the world; it endorses for us where we can feel ourselves comfortable for survival.

The social world endorses us for societal activities, comprising social, political and economic studies, which are the basic necessities of human life. These studies teach us the value of humans and humanity, which leads us to virtue, by which here prevails peace and prosperity, which are not simply important but the first and foremost necessity of humans.

The psychological world of thoughts, feelings and behavior of humans is an innovative one; the brain that the Almighty provided us works around the clock, never rests and makes humans desirous. This makes humans well aware of the purpose of life, that is, we must work for the welfare of the deprived.

It is observed that all this happens if a human makes himself Disciplined so that one may live an ethical life, but the real self-knowledge is when one thinks of the knowledge of salvation, which is the ultimate knowledge and how we may acquire it, which becomes a curiosity for humans. So, an attempt has been made to make it understandable for the reader so that we may be able to explore it more. Self-knowledge and self-realization are two terms; knowledge is good; it has a command over the subject, but the realization is divine; it requires a much deeper study of the subject. We will discuss self-realization here. Self-realization is to know about the self (the Atman). The basic fundamental is that we are the Atman, not the physical body. Since man is inherently pure and divine, every human being is potentially divine. Our first objective is the study of Atman. A human being is such a creature that we call him an explorer of the universe. The knowledge capacity of his mind moves from the deepest point of the ocean to the highest point of space, but still, the mind is busy in exploring the universe for the benefit of mankind. Our universe is so big and tedious that the knowledge we have at present is just a drop in the ocean. Similarly, to have knowledge of the self is not a simple but a rigorous study that proved to be the ultimate, as humans themselves are research entities and to explore this knowledge is the quality of the human being that we are studying here. The self-knowledge starts with two basic questions:

a. What is the object of the study?
b. What are the benefits of this study to society?

India is a country from which the seeds of spiritualism and education have been sown. The oldest and biggest text on spiritualism was written in India and is still available, the Rigveda, one of the oldest texts written in Sanskrit that still survives in the world. The archaeologist of the world has recognized and recommended this. The system of education started in India. Aryabhata (476 CE) was a master in astronomy and a mathematician who deduced the value of the "pi" and sine tables in trigonometry, which puts India at the apex of literacy and society. In Indian philosophy, the self or the soul is one, the body is a composition of matter whereas the soul is a no-matter entity. As long as the soul is in the body, a human being has to go through the materialistic activity prevailing in the universe and one must realize that a non-material entity that is supreme resides in the body. It is only the body where the soul can reside; the body is an abode for the soul. So, a self is known by Atman and the study of the self is the study of the soul along with the study of the interaction of the self with the materialistic world. The self is in the service of the soul, so it remains busy throughout the day, getting experiences for the soul, who feels every action, whether good, bad, joy, sorrow, etc. to act accordingly. To understand this entity, one has to merge with it, which means going deep into the subject, discarding the duality that arises between the mind and the field of study and controlling the mind and the body by way of obtaining the minimum and necessary requirements and maintaining silence in the mind and the body to see the experiences of the subject in which one is studying. This will experience one's, that is, the experience of one's total existence. This experience is very much reflexive in one's mind; it reflects what has happened and what one has thought. The difference in results may sometimes bring distortions in one's thinking and understanding. To overcome such distortions, the Vedic literature suggests that in such cases, one should remove the barrier that stands between you and your experience itself. One should remove all the modifications that develop in the mind, as this development is at the mental level and does not relate to the actual event. It is asserted that in order to get the totality of any experience, one has to think beyond the dualities. In this way, one can illuminate the light of self-knowledge with its own truth rather than the truth that our mind perceives through the materialistic world. This makes our character inclined toward virtuous thinking and keeps us from acting accordingly. To know more about the true nature of the self, one needs more deep study, which is the study of spirituality and ultimately this leads us to self-realization. Spirituality leads us to the truth and the truth leads to immortality, which is a soul and a question of this topic. As per the philosopher, they narrated like this: when one merges with the soul, a greater level of knowledge, wisdom and understanding is being set up, which makes us capable of designing and deciding the aspects of the physical body and also helps in exploring human spiritual evolution.

For the soul to be realized, the light of **I am** has to enter into our existence. Grace can only install the energy of **I am** and provide a base for the construction of our personal selves. Individual self-realization is a function of fusion **me** with **I am.** We must bear in mind that the **I am** here is not universal consciousness itself but rather a position of that universal energy that is transferred into our internal reality to serve as a foundation for the birth of our soul. The soul is a meeting of the personal and impersonal dimensions of our existence. **I am** her impersonal aspect. For that **I am** to become the soul, it has to absorb and integrate the consciousness of **Me** into itself. The event of becoming our soul is difficult for the linear mixed to grasp; then who becomes the soul? **I am** not the soul and **Me** is not the soul, then, yet someone have to become the soul. The miracle of the soul is this: that awakening is the event of **me** graduating from the dimension of **me** and merging into the dimension of **I am.** It is **me** that becomes the soul through its own surrender to **I am.** The bridge between **me** and **I am** is pure **me**. Pure **me** shares the qualities of both **me** and **I am** both personal and impersonal. However, it is not enough for **me** to surrender into **I am** in order for the soul to awaken. There has to be a meeting between **me** and **I am** a meeting of love and consciousness not just an energetic fusion but an activation of one's full potential. There is recognition and understanding of the event of becoming our deeper selves. Here to become means to embody the light of **I am** through the consciousness of pure **me**. The soul is who we are on a deeper level than **me**. However, to realize our soul does not mean that we cease to exist as **me.** Even though the essence of our **me** has merged into the soul, it continues to exist in its own dimension as well, but this time without forming a separate center of identity. It becomes a pure expression of the soul. **Me** is the outward face of the soul, her window into creations, her living an active principle. **Me** is the axis of the soul's intelligence and luminosity. The soul needs **me** as much as **me** need her; a bond between the two emerges in a sacred duality that constitutes the dynamics of being our higher selves. Our **me** gets fully awakened within the embrace of its higher self and an experience of soul realization happens. Only then it is pure **me** and we realize it's divinity. In its purity, **me** is an immaculate reflection of the light of creation. That is why it is allowed to merge into **I am** and give birth to our soul. We have been associated with this body and mind so closely that we have never thought about the driving force that makes the body move and the mind to think. We see that how after death, this body and mind cease to function because of the driving force behind the body and mind that has left the body. So, self-realization is knowing of the self, which means knowing of the soul and is that universal force that never dies nor takes birth, exists in every creature as a soul and resides within the body as long as the creature lives. The whole knowledge of the human being is based on the premise that man is not his body but consciousness, which is a living energy capable of self-awareness and possesses mind and memory. The body is merely a transient habitat, or man's consciousness. It is asserted that human evolution itself is the habitat of every soul, that is, dropping his old body and entering into a new one. When we study in context to death and birth, we presuppose that this is as per the will of God and also a true one, but when we study in context to the period between death and birth, the period is considered a living period where joy and sorrow both happen in the living period, which keeps us in the system of living. The human being has to go through all the phases of life and ultimately desires to move to liberation; this is the advice of our old scripture, to be followed with zeal and spirit. Everybody worships God as per their comfort, capability, conveyance and it should be kept in mind that whatever happens in life is the reward of our deeds, so humans always do as per their conscience. Everybody has their own ways to follow God, but ultimately our goal is one: "God is truth," and we must love nature which is the creation of God. Experiencing nature is experiencing God; this realizes the existence of God and by the grace of God, one keeps himself in such a state that one wishes to move to the concept of self-realization.

Self-realization is a process by which one can attain a level of oneness with the soul. The heart, which is a representative of God and the soul, becomes self-realized with the heart and one feels inseparable from God. Ramana Maharishi and others who attained the self-realization briefed on this journey of awakening, which we call self-realization, are explained as follows: Firstly, the body should be sound, not addicted to any drugs or diseases and well versed in the method of meditation, that is, sitting calmly and comfortably on a hard, stable platform in an easy mode in a room well, ventilated and concentrating your attention at one point of the body, which is generally taken between the eyebrow and your forehead. Pay attention to the meditation and start concentrating in the light of God. The journey starts and one gets to observe as it gets observed and one feels it started from the base of the spine, where an energetic force in a channel form produces light that sits slightly in front of the spine. The activation of the spiritual energy gets started in the channel and the subtle energy starts flowing through it. A deep Samadhi is required in this process of awakening and the human being moves into a deep consciousness state where the individual has no feeling of any attachment of any sort; that is, the individual loses contact with worldly matters. By and by, the subtle energy that was flowing started growing thicker and thicker, moving from the base of the spine to the crown. This is the opening of the "Crown Chakra". As it moves up it lights everything up. The energetic force continues beyond the crown to its peak, which is about a foot above the top of the head. After this "Star Chakra" opens, the energetic pathway then finally loops back down and comes to rest in its natural abode of the heart. When everything comes to its natural resting place in the heart, there is now an energetic opening in the heart area. This is what self-realization is. The heart is a spiritual entity because the soul sits in it. Self-realization is what, whether Yoga or "oneness" with truth, whether the direct perception or experience of truth, whether by knowing all intuitive faculty of the soul, it is asserted that oneness, which is the interconnectedness of all life, refers to being one with the universe, that is, to move beyond duality. We experience oneness when we are at one with God or the divine. Self-realization is, in many ways, an obscure term and its meaning is not immediately apparent. For many, it is a term that means the same as "enlighten," a word that is similar but difficult to determine. However, the term self-realization is more useful as it actually refers to a very specific stage in the journey of awakening. In most cases, it is a function of initiation from a spiritual guide. A guide is someone who has the key to unlocking this door and creating the bridge between mind and soul. So, this is an introduction to the self-realization and experiences of our great philosopher, which the writer tries to explain in his version to inspire the reader to move for salvation, which is the highest status in humanism. In reality, it's easy, but we have kept ourselves so involved in this materialistic world that it is difficult to get out of this ridiculous disease. So, to overcome this, we first have to use our will and secondly, a spiritual teacher's guidance can help us overcome this.

Our ancient literature describes a law of nature as, "I am the immeasurable potential of all that was, is and will be." Self-realization is the goal of all human endeavors and all spiritual paths. It involves the merging of the ego self, which identifies with one body, one personality, one family, one nationality, with the universal self. This realization is akin to what we experience when we awaken from a nightmare of being trapped in a small, dark place. We feel intense relief, boundless joy and gratitude for having awakened in freedom.

There are a series of challenges that a human being has to face to lead a disciplined life. Life itself is a challenge between good and evil, spirit and matter, soul and body, life and death, knowledge and ignorance, health and disease, changelessness and transitions, self-control and temptations and more. Devotees should analyze their daily mental and physical actions to determine how much their lives are influenced by the ego's ignorance and body consciousness and how much they are capable of expressing their divine nature.

Understanding the self is recognizing one's life, which means recognizing one's existence. Life itself has a purpose and that purpose is to live selflessly. When we begin to live selflessly, we align with the purpose of the universe. The universe itself is selfless, without a body, formless and without any quality. Virtuous is the physical manifestation of God. Our purpose is to realize this virtuous nature to realize the worthlessness of the physical world. To realize the formless and worthless is to realize the bodiless. To realize the bodiless is to recognize the self without any words, ego, concepts, or ideas. The attainment of this state is called Moksha, which is our true freedom.

There are three different paths to liberation (Moksha): the Path of Action (Karma Yoga), the Path of Devotion (Bhakti Yoga) and the Path of Knowledge (Jnana Yoga).

In the Path of Actions, all actions are considered Karma, as Swami Vivekananda explains. The secret of Karma Yoga is that one must perform their duty with a spirit of detachment, renouncing the fruit of their actions. It is a favored process by which one can attain perfection and it is an easy path that leads to salvation.

At present, the world is full of chaos and confusion and we too are so affected by this bad scenario that it does not seem that we will get rid of such a ridiculous disease. So, to move for Moksha, we have to overcome this in spite of the fact that we have to live in this world and even in the present scenario. This is only possible when we adopt the Path of Devotion, where hatred, jealousy, lust, anger, egoism, pride and arrogance get replaced with feelings of joy, divine ecstasy, bliss, peace and wisdom. This is the path where love exists only. Vedanta says that there is a fine thread made of pure love that connects our hearts with the divine and this thread is the essence of devotion (*Bhakti*). This has been in our hearts since our creation, as history reveals, or as we say, it is Indian hereditary, so such actions also lead to salvation.

The Path of Knowledge. It is the quest in humans that we intend to know every entity; it means we want to gain knowledge and, more correctly, say that we wish to be wise. It is the wisdom that makes us capable of discriminating between real and not real. It is said that it is a difficult path because we have to apply our minds and intellect to reach our destination. The Upanishads (*spiritual scriptures*) call it the razor's edge, where the ego is always trying to knock us off. So, to do it, we require great strength of character, willpower and intellect. Our acts should be such that they uplift the wisdom of this universe, that is, from selfish thinking to selfless thinking. It means we have attained Godhood, that is, to do God's work of maintaining or balancing this universe, to save every entity of the universe from the wrath of evil. Evil is not a person, but it is our ignorance, which we have created due to our limited knowledge and because of this lack of knowledge, we have misaligned ourselves with the universal self. It is this state when one aligns himself with the universe, that is, oneness, that is, with God; it is a Samadhi state, that is, one does not see himself in spite of all one's possessions. This ignorance is within us in the form of EGO. To recognize the selfless self, which is our real existence, The real self is what a person actually likes. The ideal self is the way in which a person would like to see himself; the self is the way in which the person sees himself now. We are universally not separate, but somehow, because of our intelligence, we have created separation, keeping aside its consequences because we cannot see the other end. We cannot see the meeting place of self with real self and that has created two, which is actually one and is active in this very moment. To create total synchronism with the self is our first purpose. It will create peace and serenity by allowing us to align our bodies, minds and emotions as one. This understanding will generate love for everyone as a self and that love will generate constructive energy to serve the universe without seeking anything in return. This must be our nature. With this unique talent of living, we can attain everlasting love, peace and happiness and realize God as our true nature (self-realization). This can be achieved only by serving oneself and everyone else. There is nobody besides me and I am nobody and that nobody is God. God is the infinite field of intelligence. We are connected to that intelligence and again, the expression of that intelligence is unconditional love. We can express our divinity only through unconditional love. We cannot master, see, hear, or feel it, but still, it touches us everywhere. It is the silence that is enveloping us all the time to protect us and make us aware of the purpose and meaning of our lives. The difference between a human being and other species is that a human being has the senses and capabilities to tame all these without disturbing the ecological system of nature, whereas the rest are for the logistical support of nature and humans. Self-realization is a way of knowing ourselves in a much better way than the way we currently know ourselves. We may know something about our thought process, our personality and our emotions; we may have been psychoanalyzed already, but still, we are lagging behind in knowing about the nature of life. Self-awareness represents credential aspects of a human being, including how one is perceived by others and its impact on society. It is the study of one's personality, which is due to one's actions in life. When one focuses on himself regarding one's personality and compares this with the prevailing environment, some defects may arise that need correction. These corrections specify how one has to think, feel and behave. We may call this the standard of self-awareness.

One's behavior must match these standards; otherwise, one feels guilty in himself, that is, in one's conscience, which won't allow one to move forward. This is the inbuilt quality in a human being that keeps one aware of not to indulge in wrong activities. To overcome this, one must change his behavior to align with these standards to feel satisfied. There are two brand categories of self-awareness:

i. **Internal Self-Awareness**. Internal self-awareness comprises the social actions (passions, aspirations) of a human being and their reactions accordingly (feelings, behavior, good or bad) in society, which leave an impression on others. It is observed that internal self-awareness leads to a quality of assurance that leads to a happy life and is a necessity for everyone.

ii. **External Self-Awareness**. External self-awareness comprises knowing about the views of others in reference to the above-mentioned social actions.

The research shows that understanding the reactions of others in this connection and acting accordingly as per norms is a skilled and wise task. It is a universal fact that our lives are full of obstacles and opportunities that we come across daily and it's the human being who, through his awareness, tackles all these to lead a comfortable and peaceful life, which is the ultimate aim of life. It becomes necessary for a human being to have experience with self-awareness, which leads one to learn how to live safely in this materialistic environment. One can get such experiences by keeping himself as involved in such events as one can devote so that these events may be fulfilled safely. To overcome such events, the mind, which makes the decision of right and wrong, plays a great role in deciding this. The mind has two stages, the conscious and subconscious stages. The subconscious stage is when one is not fully concentrating on the matter in hand, that is, when one's mind is at some other place and the work in hand is of some other nature, a contradiction in mind takes place. This situation takes place when one feels some defects in its own personality. To overcome such situations, one should make himself conscious and concentrate on the object in hand, which keeps him out of this subconscious stage. In this way, the conscious stage in the mind gets started and one begins to gain self-awareness in his mind and the subconscious stage gets eliminated. That is how the mind works and starts processing its own thoughts and emotions. It keeps one capable of controlling one's emotions and behavior, which keeps one utilizing himself in the service of mankind. As such, it keeps one conscious of one's own body and mind, which keeps one healthy, sound and environmentally friendly. It makes one capable of listening to all the participants calmly and attentively, which takes one to the purpose of the speaker and allows one to move appropriately. Listening to important people puts one within the capability of its own senses, that is, to understand the thoughts and emotions of others. It makes one capable of acting appropriately and conveniently; it is a credential aspect of one. It is asserted that to understand self-awareness, one has to study the five key components:

i. **Identifying Emotions**. A human being is an emotional being as his mind keeps the senses of feelings and emotions that are caused by an external or internal event in this interactive environment. Experiencing the nature of emotions is experiencing the situation prevailed at that moment, which leads to experiencing the self-awareness with which human beings act appropriately for appropriate results. It is the emotions that indicate the sense of the situation for which the reaction of a human being should be such that it proves to be useful to all beings; it is the experiences of a human being to sense the emotions and to act accordingly. There is no good or bad emotion, but how one acts for the emotions so that it is considered to be good, means that our actions must be analytical.

ii. Accurate self-perception, means one's judgment in assessing the quality of others in different aspects; it puts us on a distinction status; it shows the wisdom of the person; such qualities add value, as it is a credit to a person. We must have a firm decision supported by facts, not a fluctuating support of imaginary ideas; this puts one in a distinctive and productive position. So, one's actions should be like those of a performer.

iii. Recognizing strength and self-awareness, is the composition of activity today and tomorrow; this indicates the culture and strength of the organization. Awareness boosts one's confidence and increases the rate of success in life. The strength can be recognized and increased by interacting with seminars, attending conferences in the fields of literature, social science and economics, which puts the person's rating up and the ultimate strength is recognition of the organization.

iv. Possessing strong self-confidence: self-confidence comes from the culture of the organization and if the culture is associated with ethics, self-confidence is sure to happen. It is also one of the reasons for the success of the organization. Improving weaknesses and practicing successes are indicators of self-confidence. Positive attitude and transparency boost self-confidence for innovations and are incredible assets of an organization.

v. Possessing self-efficacy: means how to achieve a goal with prescribed norms; it is very much connected with self-realization; self-efficacy is a sister concern of self-realization. Self-efficacy is, by virtue of having experience in accurate self-perception, it keeps one recognizing and maintaining self-strength in all aspects; it provides and maintains the ethical culture to create self-confidence in others; and it keeps the provision to face the obstacles that sometimes arise unnecessarily by the circumstances. All this leads to a work culture that creates self-efficacy in the organization. This self-efficacy brings self-awareness to human beings at all times.

Indian epistemology or the theory of knowledge, comprises two particular terms: the study of Indian epistemology matters of common, everyday experiences (the nature of knowledge) on the one hand and the insights of cognition (the process of acquiring knowledge, the difference between true and false), the second term, that is, "jnana" and "prama". All the types of knowledge are known as "jnana" and true or valid knowledge is called "prama", whereas false knowledge is called "aprama". Epistemology is the main branch of Indian philosophy. It requires two questions to be explored: "What is the theory of knowledge" and "How is knowledge acquired". The other two branches of Indian philosophy are metaphysics, or ontology and ethics. Epistemology is the study that determines the reality of knowledge in reference to its nature, origin, range and condition. The knowledge that we acquire from ideas and the ideas that we get from beliefs and experiences may have true or false knowledge, just as beliefs may be true or false. This awareness between true and false knowledge, which is referred to as valid and invalid knowledge, made us inquire about the origin and validity of that knowledge. Epistemology maintains a systematic approach to knowledge that is solely centered on knowledge itself; therefore, epistemology is the theory of valid knowledge. In Western philosophy, Kant, a philosopher, divides the theory into two categories: conceptual knowledge and perceptual knowledge. Prior to this, there is one more knowledge, which is the knowledge of "I," that is, self-awareness. All intuitive knowledge originates from this "I" consciousness. In the dictionary, it means awakening, which is to make humans ready for any event. In Vedic theory, it is the process of evolution where one has the urge to evolve it into higher forms. It does not require its source in the conception of the mind or in sense perception; it is due to the conjunction of the self, the energy system and the potency of the thoughts of the individual.

Conceptual knowledge is an idea that reflexes in the mind and consequently is put into action by a critic. An engineer is the best example, as an engineer has to make the concept of his every work in mind and put that to concern in the form of a drawing that one can easily understand. Every work is considered unique. So, the concept of each work has to be brought into mind and reflected as per the choice of the consumer. Getting it completed as per the choice of the customer in an appropriate way is treated as the intensity of the individual making the concept. The intensity of the concept varies from person to person and depends on the hereditary structure of the individual's mind and laws of thought. The laws of thought are the fundamental guiding principles for humans' rational thinking and are empirical. Laws of thought are, firstly, the Law of Contradiction, which asserts that any statement supported by logic cannot have two or no aspects and possesses only one aspect, which is true or false. Secondly, the law of excluded middle or third states that statements supported by logic have no middle value that is either true or false; there is no middle value; logic stays only in one aspect at a time. Fourth, the principle of identity states that if any statement is true, then it is true. A statement cannot remain the same and change its truth value, as every aspect has its own identity, whatever it may be.

Perceptual Knowledge. It is tentative and suppositional knowledge and needs someone to justify it. A philosophy is the study of the fundamental nature of humans and the material involved in living, which puts one in a comprehensive system of ideas and allows one to engage, analyze and put their ideas in public for open criticism. Every philosopher has their own thinking and vision and puts their theories as per their logic accordingly. Some say reasons are the criteria that make one think about finding logic for the reasons that lead one to a source of knowledge acquisition We call this rational knowledge. Some say experiences are the source of acquiring knowledge. Experiencing means acquiring knowledge through interactions with events, so the more interactions, the greater the knowledge, which involves actions. We call this empirical knowledge. Some say knowledge is a God-given entity and whatever knowledge one has acquired is all by the grace of God, but it is a wrong belief, as divine literature suggests and a universal fact that one's Karma is one's destiny. So, believing in God is good, but it's your Karma that makes your status and destiny and what the Karma is: "one's any action is one's Karma". The foremost Karma for a human being is acquiring rational knowledge with proper norms, which makes the human being an ideal one. Epistemologists analyze the concept of knowledge and come to the conclusion that epistemology has three main conditions: belief, truth and justification. Belief is the mind's exercise that brings knowledge into the human's mind. The mind has a belief in that knowledge, which has no evidence, so the beliefs may not always be correct or accurate. In spite of knowing all these, our lives are driven by belief, as belief is such an entity to whom we believe and accept as true; therefore, knowledge is a sort of belief. To acquire certain knowledge, an environment pertaining to that knowledge has to be created; that is, some beliefs have to be adopted in mind regarding that knowledge, which may be true or false. It is then the mind that clarifies these beliefs by way of acquired knowledge and experiences, which put one in a state of accepting or rejecting that knowledge. But when one tries to seek rational knowledge, our beliefs approach the right attitudes and may become a source of true knowledge.

Truth. It must be in our minds that we are presuming a rational aspect of knowledge, which means that truth is a condition of knowledge. If there is no truth, then we cannot constitute knowledge. So, to gain knowledge, truth is the basic concept to be undertaken for the acquisition of knowledge. Knowledge and truth are both interrelated; the truth does not require any proof that it is true. Truth means a true proposition and there is no justification to prove its sanctity because the base of knowledge is truth.

Justification is to make the knowledge most authentic, necessary logic and evidence are required to support that knowledge, which is the right way to call it justifiable knowledge. The evidence, based beliefs and potency of the evidence constitutes the true and justification level of that knowledge. So, logic and evidence are the parameters to justify the knowledge.

Epistemology and Metaphysics. Epistemology is the theory of knowing the source of knowledge, whereas metaphysics is the theory of the credential aspects of knowledge; it is concerned with the conditions of validity of knowledge; metaphysics investigates the reality of nature. It is observed that generally research work (metaphysics) is being done on those matters whose fundamental base has already been initiated, that is, epistemology philosophy, which is in process. This shows that epistemology and metaphysics are interrelated. The object of epistemology is the study of the definition of real knowledge, the determination of what the nature of reality is, whereas the object of metaphysics is the study of an ideal of knowledge, that is, what does it mean to exist? The method of gaining knowledge in epistemology is the study of ideas and beliefs, whereas the method of study in metaphysics is the practical investigation of existence. According to Dr. Ward, epistemology is a systematic reflection concerning knowledge that takes knowledge itself as the object of science. The function of knowledge is to consolidate and complete random and incomplete concepts into a systematic and universal form that is useful for human activity.

In Indian philosophy there are six parameters as correct means of acquiring knowledge: perception, inference, comparison and analogy, postulation, derivation from circumstances, non-existence and authority of words. All the knowledge is from beliefs; beliefs may be true or false; the justification makes them true or false; the truth is, which satisfies the masses considering all the parameters of the nature of knowledge. The nature of knowledge is the theory of knowledge that our philosophers try to explore from time-to-time in response to the environment at that time. This accumulation of knowledge is still insufficient for human beings, as everyone has their own thinking and ideas, which leads philosophers to go deep into the subject. This results in the availability of more and more literature for studying and pointing out the deficiencies. This process has been carried out since humans started the research on nature, which is living proof. This shows that knowledge has no end but only a beginning whenever and anytime one gets it started. Perception here refers to sense perception; the justification between right and wrong refers to sense perception. True perception arises when the internal object (intuition), which appears in the form of awareness and the external object, which is in touch with the senses, are identical. The resultant awareness is called perception. Perception, as a source of knowledge, is an individual belief and is dependent on the concept; the concept is an image of the object that is under investigation. The concept is a composition of knowledge and experience that leads one to the destination. This shows that concept-laden presumptions are not only the ability of the senses but also the capacity of the mind, which is the type of cognition that may result in a good target. It is the quality of the mind that memorizes the real concept and acts as a source of knowledge as and when needed. So, perception is a belief and belief is a source of operation for perception, which acts as a source of knowledge.

Inference is the combination of truth and observation; knowledge without truth is invalid knowledge. In inference, we consider the truth. A true event is like a smoke coming out of the jungle, which means a fire has been broken up in the jungle. Secondly, considering true observations by quoting reasons makes one capable of acquiring knowledge. In this way, inference gives us a source of knowledge. In Indian texts, inference is explained in three parts: hypotheses, reasons and examples. The hypothesis is further divided into two parts:

whether that idea needs investigation or not and whether that idea is affirmed. Inference as a source of knowledge is based on logic that makes it easy to understand the facts, but it does not act as a source of knowledge generation. Hypothesis means a fact that is out of reach of the senses, just as an atom of the body is a composition of small atoms of earth, water, air, fire and sky. It is a fact, but we cannot sense it as it is a natural, endless process. Second is the existence of God. It is a fact that God exists everywhere, but we cannot see it because it is formless. Thirdly, in the scientific process, the hypothesis is made before any research work is to be done. Reasons are the source of knowledge; adductive reasoning is a form of logical inference in which we consider the set of observations and find the simplest and most likely conclusion from the observations. The process yields a probable conclusion. Informal reasoning (data-based) proved to be the best source of knowledge for making decisions in challenging activities. The inference knowledge is taken as valid when positive examples are being put as evidence, such as if smoke comes out of a jungle, it infers that fire has been broken out in a jungle as smoke and fire are correlated to each other, so it acts as true evidence.

Comparison and Analogy are the study of proving the best option among the similarities of two or more different entities. One can derive the knowledge of similarity between two entities. It is the study of heuristic values. It is the source of knowledge, which is based on the analysis of reasoning and evaluating analogical thinking, which then refers to the process of transferring knowledge from one particular entity (the source) to another entity (the target). In other words, the interaction between the base (the source), a set of representational entities and the target (the target), a set of outcomes of representational entities, by comparing only the specific properties of the element, the analogy only identifies a selective set of properties.

Analogical thinking is a specific way of thinking based on the idea of utilizing and practicing existing knowledge to generate insights and formulate the best possible solutions to problems. In this way, an idea is developed to counter the problem and acts as a source of knowledge. Most sources of knowledge are by way of cognitive processes, which are broader than analogical reasoning and lead to cognitive science research, which indicates the good character of the study.

Postulation and Derivation from Circumstances. Postulation means the suggestions from the existing knowledge and derivation from the circumstances as the word perceives it means the circumstantial implication. The study suggests that every entity is a category and appropriate methods are applied for interpreting and representing the category, which makes us capable of understanding the problems and can be applied in a discipline by applying the existing available knowledge. Keeping this in mind, consider the waste of energy in Higher Education Institutions (HEI). To overcome this problem, two aspects have to be considered: the behavior of the consumer and the implications of energy-saving instructions. The study reveals that students studying in higher education are more likely to waste energy than household consumers. Secondly, the study reveals that there was no such study course in the institution regarding solar energy. The students who are not conversant with consumption keep putting the concern to tackle the problem as it is their business; the students are not concerned with this. The researchers make it possible to find out the point of trouble by putting their attention deep into the subject to come out of this problem. This case may be studied and commented on accordingly. Here the entity is “energy saving in HEI” and the category is “ignorance of knowledge”, The derivative from the circumstances is to derive “energy saving”. Hence, the knowledge of energy consumption among the students in HEI is required to be assessed. This research analyzes the demand for energy among the students and an estimate of the requirement and savings can be established. Appropriate qualitative and quantitative methods are proposed to assess the energy consumption in the HEI environment. These exercises help us analyze the behavior of energy consumption and may prove useful in designing a model of energy consumption. This will also help us understand the behavior of people and their reactions to energy consumption. In this way, we get the experience to work out such problems, which ultimately becomes a source of knowledge.

Non-Existence. The concept of non-existence is a self-sufficiency concept, as non-existence is the opposite of existence. Existence, which has a sense and can be put into research work, cannot be ignored and requires analysis. The concept of non-existence was seen in ancient texts in context to objects, the object which has existence, quality and quantity; existence means explorable and can be put to analysis; quality means the property of the object in context to scientifically, philosophically and socially; quantity means macroscopic or microscopic. When we think of an object, it means to think of an existent object. As non-existence has existence in reference to an object, the object can be studied and the study confirms its existence and acts as a source of knowledge. In this way, non-existence acts as a negative term in contrast to positive terms of existence, though these negative terms are due to positive terms of existence; therefore, these negative terms also have existence, quality and quantity and can be studied, such as form of testimony, theory of causation and analysis of deficits as real and valuable.

Authority of Words. It's the word that puts the human being as high as the sky and the human being as low as the earth; it reflects the credential aspects of the human being. Hence, the words are the authority of the validity and non-validity of an entity. A word is defined as a word that has the capacity to convey its meaning. The concept of the word means relying on testimony. There is a quest in human beings to gain knowledge, at least where one has competition with others to prove supremacy and, moreover, to pace with the environment for a legitimate living. It is the word whether these may be written or spoken that reflects the educational credential aspects of the human being and acts as a source of knowledge. The potency of the word to convey its meaning comes from the reliability of the source. The reliability of the source is an important issue and must be taken into consideration, as true knowledge is only derived from reliable sources. The Vedas are considered to be the perfect and oldest scripture, so they act as a reliable source of knowledge.

CHAPTER - 4

Philosophy

E**thics**. The base of ethics is truth, the truth that also stands for eternal and eternal means to whom we sense forever. It means the philosophy of ethics is eternal and its concept teaches us the way of life; the life that is a part of the universe acts as a medium to explore its creativity and beauty. Ethics put us in contact with consciousness and self-awareness, which conferred our connection to the universe. As in spirituality, consciousness is the basic form of having a connection with the cosmos, which puts both the interdependent and inter relations to each other. So, it is asserted that there is no life without the universe and the universe has no value without living life. Ethics is the art of living toward living and non-living things, which is a foundation for human beings as it is the human being who has interaction with the surroundings, whether they are living or non-living, as everything in the universe is for a certain purpose and has utility, so every entity has importance of their own accord. The study of living and non-living are both important for human beings, as living is not possible without the logistic support of non-living; therefore, it becomes our moral duty to protect and save nature's gift to human beings. Our environment, nature's biggest gift to human beings, that is, the plants and trees, the water, etc. are essentials for human beings by which life becomes possible to exist on this planet. So, to use these and to protect them ethically is our first and foremost duty, considering the subjectivity and objectivity of our actions toward any entity. The objective of our ethics toward any entity is that "our actions must suit all." It's true that action is life and life without action is death. So, our actions are beneficial for society and the environment. Consider the case of plants and trees. Nature has provided us with plants and trees to save our lives, whereas these are the only source of wood for construction activities and are also a source of wooden fire, which acts in performing social and customary rites. The main function of the trees and plants that save our lives is to release polluted free air for the creatures for their living and absorb polluted air released by all creatures by their activities. So, we ourselves should assess how useful trees are for all of us and then it becomes our primary duty to protect and save them. Sometimes, it becomes imperative that trees be cut and then it also becomes our duty to plant the trees in double numbers so that at least they may grow as much in number as they have been cut. This is the objective of ethics in the case of plants and trees; it suits all, is beneficial for all and is also a fact. Subjectivity is the personal belief or feeling of the person making the judgment regarding the activity in question. Let us consider plants and trees and how they should be treated. In their views, plants and trees are the best source of generating revenue, but mark a question with an old saying: "wood is good, but trees are better" and if we consider these in context to health "trees are life". So, wealth is not to be considered appropriate against trees and in context to health, trees should not be cut. Therefore, in every action, objectivity and subjectivity are to be taken into consideration, which will boost the vision of the person. Ethics makes the human being a conscious one, which means one must presuppose the concept in relation to the ideology of the object, which must be taken into consideration before any decision is taken.

With the passage of time and with the foolishness of people, it happened since ancient times that the war of ego got started, resulting in a change in dynasty and with the change in dynasty, there was a change in literature. As the old saying goes, "as the king, so is the people", every dynasty put his own philosophy, such as in the case of the Greeks. Ancient history reveals that the Greeks took ethics as a matter of routine jobs and as a result, everyone may do the work as per his own will, so this did not last long. So, the philosopher realized that ethics as an eternal thing must have due importance and have a role in life as it puts us in a context of virtues, which is the essence of happiness and excellence. Happiness accounts for "good life for humans," excellence accounts for moral virtues and happiness and finally, virtues of character account for two aspects. Firstly, the evaluation of people must be distinct as per their actions, that is, it must be based on their character rather than their theoretical justifications. Secondly, it seems that people used to be more conscious of their character than their moral knowledge, so it is asserted that emphasis should be placed on virtue of character as it leads to a good life. The Romans, in this context, took ethics as a force to govern the law; their ethics were full of sternness. The strict discipline makes them able to govern the universe. The Romans were well disciplined in socialism and the mind, which made their system powerful; it kept their dynasty alive longer than the Greeks but could not last due to imperfections in their ideals. The Chinese took the eternal in higher aspects and considered it a creation of God. The Chinese assert that God is omnipresent and that whatever we observe in this universe is the creation of God and that too in the interest of mankind. The Chinese follow the divine's law and literature, in which respect for parents is the highest devotion to God and this gives an idea of governing; the people who serve the people, like the parents, are the governing ethics for the organization.

To follow norms in every activity, duties of their daily lives and manners were the main characteristics of the Chinese.

The ancient Aryans of India stood above all these as they had the ideas of truth: truth is God, God in himself, God in man and God in nature were the views of their lives. The literature of Indian civilization was intellectual, an ideal one and in reference to reasoning, which boosted the recognition of ethical literature. The Indian literature on ethics in every aspect is available and can be put to use comfortably to avoid violations; this enhances a tense, free life. The character and culture of Indians are warmed and softened with emotional and spiritual meaning and broad knowledge of the soul as compared with Roman character and culture, which are hard, cold, narrow and without any touch of the spirit in man. This shows that Indian culture is so intellectual and logical that no other culture stands. In Indian ethos, there are social as well as individual ethics. Social ethics refer to your conduct in relation to the society, whereas individual ethics refer to your conduct in relation to other members of the society. It may be ethical or unethical, as this is an individual relationship between me and him. There may be a difference in incompatibility, whereas societal ethics have a common objective: one can submit his suggestion, not the decision. Both ethics constitute ethical life and proved to be useful as per their convenience of time and place. Societal ethics are useful for all, so one should consider it a duty toward others and therefore given the name of the "ethics of doing" whereas individual ethics are the personal judgment of the individual, it may be right or wrong, it analyzes the inner sense of the human being but it also plays a good role. An experienced person is required who gets it possible to solve the problem, therefore, we call this the "ethics of being". It is observed that ethical persons are preferred and given importance on any occasion of sorts; this is the identity of ethics and one feels satisfaction, considering this a reward of one's conduct. It is observed that an ethics-abiding individual has the habit of always speaking the truth, adhering to not stealing, never taking bribes, fully utilizing the time and going on doing his duty earnestly and fearlessly.

Some fundamentals for individual ethics are performing one's duty, performing duty to the best of ability is only possible when there is no stress on the mind of any sort and is the foremost act of the individual. The duty must involve commitment to the target, accountability for results, an ideal for others and a character for society. Performing duty to the best is the understanding of the wellness of society and the organization. Honesty is one of the constituents of ethics, it is presumed that ethics exists there, where honesty prevails. It is an old saying that "honesty is the best policy of life," so to live prosperously and peacefully, honesty is the key to success. An honest person always follows good behavior, is truthful, maintains discipline and possesses a good attitude toward others. Working with honest people reflects a charming environment, as it enables us to make better decisions and puts us in a fruitful state, thus satisfying our conscience. So, to be honest, this is a good credential aspect of a human being. Vision is the quality of a person's ability to generate innovative ideas for the betterment of society.

Vision, is the future of being and motivates the concerns to reach the destination. It was the vision of our leadership that our leaders took the foremost decision of framing the constituent of India, which is based on a certain moral vision that brings liberalism to society, a vision of Rammohan Roy. A vision of social justice within orthodox Hinduism, introduced by K. C. Sen, Justice Ranade and Swami Vivekananda, could not be possible without liberty. So, our constituent is the longest, most descriptive in the world and shows the vision of our literary culture. Vision, which makes a sense of leadership to whom the majority follows, means a sign of success, which must be the foremost goal of an organization.

Balanced one, human being is said to be a balanced human being when their every action possesses discipline and morality in order to satisfy others or be liked by valued persons. A balanced person senses the emotions of others and acts accordingly. It is observed that a balanced person is well versed in spirituality and materialism, so they follow the principle that "health is wealth". It is only possible when our environment, that is, ecology, remains in a balance that we are rigorously trying to pollute, by which unbalanced conditions have been developed, causing variations in the weather and leading to distortion. As humans are very much connected with the environment, it affects the physical condition of the person; that is, the deterioration in health of the person is being observed. In such conditions, if one keeps himself in a balanced state, such a human being becomes an ideal for others and boosts enthusiasm among others to become a balanced human being. It must be the characteristics of an ethical person.

Self-learning, is the quality in people that some people are curious to learn and our day-to-day work has become the best source of learning which we call experiences. It is asserted that taking different works means more experience and means more knowledge, so we conclude that we can gain learning from experiences and these experiences are through our actions, in which our lively involvement includes, it is our action in socialism and materialism. Diversity is an opportunity to develop skills in various modes which gives us aid in delivering our duties of living and keeps us an aware human beings.

Self-confidence, is a feeling of trust in one's capability and makes one vital. One gains capability through education and experience which makes one a self-confident human being. There is no time for acquiring knowledge unless and until there is a will for learning. So learning is at the level of the individual which is the foremost indicator of self-confidence and second are the experiences that one gets by accepting the challenges. Indians have the quality of facing and accepting the challenges, which keeps them at the apex. So Indian leaders stood at the apex of the world as they have a record of not initiating any type of war with anyone and treating the world as one family till date; this shows their self-confidence. A confident person brings comforts at home, at work and in relationships. Self-confidence is the lifeline of organizational success.

Patience, is a virtue that has proven to be useful at all times and the possession of this quality in a human being gives one the credit of "wise man". Patience is controlling the emotions of oneself by putting himself in a calm and peaceful state in hazardous situations and using wisdom to seek peace and reconciliation. Patience keeps the individual smiling in spite of knowing one has a hard time ahead of him. Patience is a vital quality in leadership of any sort, as it helps the incumbent solve problems and avoid conflicts. The study reveals that growth in technology has given patience an over-dated virtue; it also reveals that having patience in competitive studies remains beneficial in the end. The present scenario is very harsh and running very fast; everyone wants to keep pace with this state, whereas it is observed that it ends with fatal diseases and puts us in an anxiety state. So, it becomes important to develop the concept of patience among other people also. It also gives us a stress-free and disease-free life; it is understood to be a prosperous life and a desire of everyone.

Self-control and restraint in speech: self-control means keeping oneself in a balanced state. The balanced state of a human is that state in which one recognizes the good and evil forces of life. This helps us to make use of the good and we consider this state a wise state of one, whose words and deeds remain the same. The wise people are those who speak less and act more, respect others and their suggestions and do not boost themselves as wise men. The words they use have their meaning in logic; they are not forced to accept them but rather to make them understand. So, the words have the power to change the situation; even if the government changes, it may prove good or bad later on. Therefore, speaking cautiously and realizing the power of words should be taken as a priority; the speech of the speaker should be true, relevant, dignified and astute. Differentiate between right and wrong. Ethics makes one understand the difference between right and wrong. The right is as per law; the law that governs the universe is called the law of right. The law of right is the law of divine law, which is considered to be supreme and adhered to by the people by setting a line of standards of right and wrong as per our old scripture and suggestions made by society. This is accepted by all as the basis of right and wrong; it is as per the reasons and the facts. The wrong is something one has committed contrary to the law. It is a universal fact that man is a composition of moral grammar; our parents and teachers act as catalysts and make us capable of generating and following moral laws. Philosophers divide ethical theory into three components: meta-ethics, normative ethics and applied ethics.

Meta-ethics is the study of the origin of ethics and the meaning of ethical concepts.

Normative ethics is the study of moral judgments, the criteria for what is right or wrong and its consequences for others.

Applied ethics, which concerns standards for right and wrong behavior and looks at controversial topics like war, rights and capital punishment, is a good tool for thinking about moral issues.

Meta-ethics covers issues ranging from moral semantics (investigation on the meaning of moral) to moral epistemology (how moral knowledge is possible) and prominently covers two issues: metaphysical issues and psychological issues.

Metaphysical issues related to whether morality exists independently for humans or not. Metaphysics is the study of the kinds of things that exist in nature and holds that moral values are objectives with the view that they exist in a spirit-like realm. Philosophers asserted that it is eternal or absolute and never changes its aspects. So, it is eternal, bound by eternal laws and exists independently. An evident example explained by Plato is that in mathematical relations, we have 1+1=2. This can't be changed; one can apply it anywhere in the universe and one can't alter it. Plato explained the eternal character of mathematics by stating that they are "abstract entities" that exist in a spirit-like realm. Some philosophers consider metaphysics a study of skeptical philosophical tradition and deny the status of objectivism as moral value. They asserted that it is a human concept that depends on the capability and culture of the human being. They deny the status of absolute and universal as they assert that moral values in fact change from society to society throughout the world by citing examples such as an attitude about polygamy, homosexuality and human sacrifice.

Psychological issues are related to the mind as moral judgment and conduct are based on the mind. But which understanding motivates us to be moral" is yet to be known. Though genetically one knows that killing is bad and stealing is immoral, one acts accordingly. If one is aware of this basic concept then one does not think that there is a necessity of enforcing such psychological acts. Morality and immorality are both concepts of the mind and it is the mind of the human being that makes use of these concepts for the betterment of the self and society. Betterment is that which is acceptable to all, but a human being is such a creature that one's has the quality of selfishness and it is to be noted that almost all one's actions are connected with some selfish desires. As such, one used to act as per his betterment, that is, which suits the individual, though one knows that this is a temporary betterment, but one's selfishness, which one has enforced in his mind by which one's is committed to act accordingly. This selfishness sometimes we experience so openly that, to get power over other people, one offers donations to a charity to become an active member of that charity. This view is called "psychological egoism". This shows that self-interest motivates one's to such an extent that one acts accordingly. It is to be noted that the human being also has the inherited quality of showing benevolence to others. This view is called psychological altruism. This shows that a human being is not only selfish, but one's actions are also instinctive benevolence. So, in my view, "to be moral" is the state of mind at the time and place of action, not hereditary. Normative ethics, or meta-ethics is the formulation of ethical standards; normative ethics is for its regulation; it may be one rule or a set of rules. There must be ideal standards and their consequences for every act, it comprises virtue theories, duty theories and consequentiality theories. According to virtue theories, an ideal person is considered a virtue person as the ideal person possesses the qualities of good morality which we get evident by one's acts as per words and deeds. It places stress on developing good habits and character. It is asserted that good habits make us good in all aspects. Virtue theory holds that we should avoid acquiring bad character traits and emphasizes moral education, which helps us in regulating the discipline at work and makes us active for common causes such as benevolence. The quality of benevolence makes us always rational and is a practical truism. It is generally observed that good intentions are the intention to act well and to do right in any given situation; this is what we call practical wisdom, that is, the knowledge or understanding that the possessor acts to do acts in any given situation. So, virtue is not simply "goodness" but a determination to always act right.

According to duty theories, a human being's life is full of duties that one has to perform without considering the consequences but which are obligatory. Considering the duty toward one's children, one has to take care of one's children right from birth until their ability to stand independently in every aspect. This is an obligation on human beings, as sometimes it is observed that the grown children proved not to be fit for society. In spite of this, one has to obey this duty, whatever the consequences. The duty theories are classified into four components: duties to God, duties to himself, duties to others and absolute duties. The philosopher asserted that duty to God comprises knowing the existence of God, the nature of God and worshiping God by heart. So, to comply with these, God enables the human being to obey God's commandments and instructions; that is, the human being is in charge of controlling, guarding and conserving the creation of God; that is, humans get entitled to marriage for the growth of the species. This puts the human toward rational thinking and keeps one to the status of a busy, tough and purposeful life performer. It gets one to enjoy or be in trouble, but we say this is the cycle of life that we have to perform and is obligatory on human beings. Duties to himself have concern with the duties of one's toward the soul and toward the body. The duty toward the soul is the development of one's talent, that is, one's actions must be rational and true to the word. The duty toward the body is not to harm the body by keeping all actions mentally strong enough that they may not hurt the body. One should be aware of what is good and bad for the body. Duties toward others are concerned with those duties that are universally binding on the human being, such as not to harm anyone; we call it an absolute duty. Absolute duty is of three sorts. Firstly, avoid blaming others; secondly, people should be duly honored and good things should be honored. One more is the conditional duty, which is an agreement between the two peoples. Conditional duty involves abiding by the promise made between the two peoples. Secondly, the duty-based approach to ethics is the right theory; the right theory is the justified claim of one's in reference to another. Such as my right is that I may not be harmed by others and towards others is that I may not harm others. The rights and duties are related to each other in such a way that the rights of one's become the duties of others. This is called the correlativity of rights and duties. Philosophers asserted that there are natural laws such as one should not harm anyone in any aspect that may bring un comfort to others and is contrary to law, so we call this a natural right; then there are universal rights, such as rights of speech, which remains the same throughout the universe; inflammatory speeches are treated as crimes against humanity; then there are equal rights; we all have equal rights to live; and then there are inalienable rights, which means one can't hand over one's rights to another, such as by selling myself into slavery; it is a legal crime and accepted by all cultures and creeds. Thirdly, duty is based on theory, emphasizing a single principle of duty. Even though there are more fundamental principles of duties, the duties that encompass one's particular duties are single self-evidence-bound. We call this duty a "categorical imperative" duty. A categorical imperative means if we want to remain fit, we need a sports activity. Here, sports activity is a categorical imperative duty that keeps us fit and then there are moral duties that are obligations on us but to which we are not legally bound, such as helping the needy, earning by fair means, duty toward society, nation, etc. We have to follow this maximum and it is to be noted that these actions are governed by the mind, so acting maximum are the actions of the mind, which too are subjective as these actions are the personal feelings of one. One does this without considering the consequences which shows one's moral worth. In this way categorical imperatives help one regulate the morality of actions and affect one's life. Fourth, it is a duty-based theory; it emphasizes prima facie duties, which literally means that at first sight, it appears to be true. In law schools, the word is used for evidence and is accepted unless it proves to be false. The philosopher urges that all our duties are part of the fundamental nature of the universe, such as fidelity, the duty to keep one's promise fulfilled. Reparation is the duty to compensate when one harms another. Gratitude is the duty to give thanks when we are being helped by others. Justice, the duty to recognize merits, Beneficence is the duty to improve the condition of others. Self-improvement is the duty to improve one's virtue and intelligence. Nonmaleficence, the duty not to hurt others, may be more to consider. In this duty-based theory, the word prima facie arises when there are conflicting situations, as it takes two to make the conflict; in such situations, one has to choose the best one. The theory can be understood through an example: suppose one has to make payments to another with the pretext that if one does not return the same amount on the due date, the other will charge the extra interest at the rate of 18% per annum. The one becomes unable to make payments on the due date on the ground that one's father becomes serious and could not go to work to fetch money. In this context, one's appeals may be that the agreement date may be extended in view of the circumstances. In this case, what duty will others act in such situations? In my view, the lender may have a nonmaleficence duty, that is, not to hurt others and the borrower should show gratitude to the lender for such an act. Consequential theory is the theory where one must know the consequences of their actions and if the actions are morally right, then the consequences seem to be more favorable. It is also a fact that every action has reactions; it is called a consequence and the consequences of one's conduct are the ultimate basis for any judgment about the rightness or wrongness of that conduct. Consequentialism is an ethical theory where the morality of an action is to be judged solely by its consequences. It states that everyone has a right to choose the work as per one's own will, but one's action must produce the greatest amount of good for the greatest number of people.

The most common form of consequentialism is utilitarianism. The word utilitarianism has a very clear meaning: the best utility of one's action. This means that one's actions must promote well-being for all. The characteristic of utilitarianism is proper orientation and thinking, which enhances well-being and a better future, which is a necessity for a human being. Utilitarianism is an ethical theory that holds good for social, rational and scientific perspectives. "Social" stands for egalitarian, meaning the well-being of every person, considering everyone is of equal value. "Rational" stands for positive thinking, based on reasons rather than emotions, thereby enhancing well-being. "Scientific" stands for logic, meaning every action can be derived and applied to enhance the utility of any entity.

Types of Utilitarianism. Act utilitarianism determines the consequences on a case-by-case basis, deciding whether the action taken is morally right or wrong based on its specific circumstances. Hedonistic utilitarianism assesses actions by their consequences, considering whether those consequences are pleasurable or painful.

Act Utilitarianism, one should focus on the value of time; time spent on leisure activities is a waste of time. Leisure is a sound emitted from the heart, processed in the mind and available to one in the shape of one's desire. Desires have no limits and are a cause of one's death. So, minimizing the desires means minimizing the leisure activities, which means utilizing the time to the best of the possibilities. This proved to be thinking of the well-being of the individual, which is morally a right act. Sometimes enforcing rules that are socially banned but proved to be useful in enforcing on children, we may call this rule utilitarianism. The child, whose mind is very sharp and not well versed in the materialistic activities of the universe, proved to be useful if the child was assigned the job as per his own will, keeping in view the behavioral code and moral rights of the child. It is observed that this proved to be a successful assignment for the child, as the child in whom the habit of stealing is common can be eliminated to a great extent. In this way, by ignoring the merit of the child in context to banned rules and adopting such actions that eliminate the one from such a ridiculous habit of stealing, an act of favorable consequences for everyone must be adopted.

Second, Hedonistic Utilitarianism, it is observed that one thinks himself morally fit when one is happy or pleasant. It means that it is the pleasure that keeps one morally fit; morally fit means societal fit; societal fit means "a well lived life". So, to be happy is the only entity that makes one valuable; this is due to our approach to doing the right thing. A right action is that which brings more happiness to the concerns. But this does not happen in all acts; other morally significant consequences may not necessarily be pleasing or painful. For example, take the act "honesty is the best policy", is a very valued act, but it may not please everyone. So, to overcome this problem philosophers propose ideal utilitarianism, which means benefiting the maximum number. It is observed that comparing the consequences of any act proved to be successful and acting accordingly gives us the ways to get the maximum number to be benefited. Philosophers also propose preference utilitarianism, where preference means desire, the action that satisfies most people, means the action is right, but the right and wrong are known through the consequences, so it is our capability to get maximize the good for people, that is, the consequences that proved to give more goods to people. This is called Preference Utilitarianism.

Applied ethics is the branch of ethics that deals with controversial issues at the national level, such as environmental issues, medical issues, animal issues, etc. The applied ethics may be applied mainly in two circumstances:

i. There are at least two groups of people, the issue must be controversial, one in favor of the issue and the other in opposition to the issue.

ii. The issue must be a distinctively moral one, such as forest conservation, energy conservation, the public versus private health care system, etc.

All these issues are also controversial because they have an impact on society as these are the logistics for life and life is very much connected with society. Though these issues are moral but there are suggestions from all walks of life and it must be. This gives us an opportunity for improvement in context to issues and a better utility can be made possible by such acts. So, to make society morally as well as socially strong, we must follow rational suggestions that strengthen the laws and become ideal for society. It is observed that wherever two groups emerge as contestants for an issue and put their claims as the correct ones. It is observed that the issue remains as it was; egoism emerges in the issue, so the issues are likely to be solved by a third group, who may act by putting the logistics first, which may eliminate egoism and thus lead to a solution to the controversy. The applied ethical theory may be applied in resolving such issues. It is not difficult to solve the issue as per the normative principle, which is based on logic it is a part of the ethical theory, which is based on consequences and a duty-based approach. Personal benefits and social benefits are the consequentiality of right actions, as they depend on the right and rational thoughts of the individual or society, whereas benevolence, honesty, etc. are the duty toward mankind.

The essence of ethics contains both a view of life and a way of life which are related to life science and social science, respectively and act as guides for the human's life. Our view of life is that we are here to learn which leads to a happy life according to our own will. It is asserted that learning starts in our lives from the day we are born and continues throughout our lives. It never gets completed, as humans always remain enthusiastic about learning more and more, an unending process. The Vedic view of life is based on the holistic science of life, declaring reality as the wholeness of creation and the oneness of self. Here, reality is seen as a human being with a holistic approach, which means relating to or concerned with integrated wholes or being complete. A person's situation is understood in relation to the whole person, including their body, emotions, mind, spirit and the whole person is seen in relation to the world. The self is our Atman and it is just a holographic image of Parmatman or infinite bliss. The self (Atman) gives life to the body and is an imperishable one. The body in which five senses reside first is the physical body which enables a human being to interact with the physical world so it is called world consciousness. Second is the soul, which shows the intelligence in the human being, which makes the existence of a human being, the generation of love and affection, all these are qualities in a human being, so it is called self-consciousness. Third is the spirit; spirit is the energy that is produced by the food that we take. We breathe and we also take food. Both go to our every cell, where the food burns with the help of the air we have taken in by breathing, resulting in generations of energy and makes us becoming a living, active physical organism. Spirit, in which human beings communicate with God, worship God and understand self-realization, comprises spirit, so it is called God consciousness. Fourth is the mind, which may be viewed as being constituted by five basic components: manas, ahamkara, citta, budhi and Atman, which cannot be reduced to a single element. The manas, or middle level of mind, obtains its input from the senses of hearing, touch, sight, taste and smell; its perception changes from moment to moment. Ahamkara is the human ego; its evaluation and decisions are made by budhi, the intellect. Manas, ahamkara and budhi are collectively called the "internal instruments" of the mind. Citta is consciousness, the memory bank of the mind and acts as a foundation for the operation of the mind. The creation of innovation and diverse emotional states occurs in this stage. Atman is consciousness; the self, or God, can be called the Atman. The mind is a complex entity; these aspects are to be taken into consideration to understand the behavior of the mind. The Vedic philosopher (Rishis) developed the system of living, the most powerful tool, "our mind," with a view to transcending the mind and experience to the human being for a good cause. Then, the heart is not simply an important physical organ of the body but a spiritual entity and a representative of God and the soul in the micro and macrocosms of God's creation.

So, the heart has many dimensions. The heart is the seat of the self as per Vedic text; when we refer to ourselves, we refer to the heart. The heart is not just the source of our existence; it is the place of unity and connection with God. Even the generation of the cosmic force dwells within the heart. The heart is the core of our being, where we experience our own self-being and, through it, the nature of the universe. The heart has great significance both as a seat where the soul rests and as a place of the abode of God. The heart has five openings and is a vital organ of the body by which one gets nourished by the soul and keeps one alive. The heart also has several veins, which go not only to other parts of the body but beyond and play an important role in procreation as a part of its energy is said to go into the formation of semen. The heart has thousands of arteries through which energy (prana or soul) flows; the soul escapes from the body into space, that is, the space between heaven and earth, at the time of death, as per our Karma. The heart is a source that connects your pious heart with the love of God through duty, knowledge, devotion, surrender, service, sacrifice and silence the love that radiates in all directions and touches anyone and everyone who comes into contact with it. As the sun radiates light, its very essence is that it touches everything in its path. The heart is a source of tremendous knowledge and a source of truth. Self-realization arises from the heart, as it is an abode of God.

The heart, as the center and support of all existence, is the source of our entire being, the ultimate source of speech and when we speak truly, we speak from the heart; the blessing too is from the heart. A human being is one who has a progressive view of life and does not worry so much about the ephemeral requirements of substance; they rather focus on finding out the meaning of life and work toward that aim. Such human beings are civilized and their lifestyle is based on spiritual culture. Human beings have no comments on the wonders of the God that we observe daily, that is, about the mystery of creation and destruction, life and death, about the forces of nature that we play daily and about the mystery of his own existence, how this is happening without end. The Indian scientist (Rishis) searched deep into in understanding the above terms, exploring the inner being through meditation and other techniques to reach the destination and came to the conclusion, which is very briefly explained in our sacred text, the Srimad Bhagavad Gita, which is an extract of divine knowledge is as follows: firstly, this universe has no beginning and no end; it is an endless process; it is eternal; that is, it was, it is and it will remain functioning as per omnipotent God's norms. Secondly, one who has come into this universe has to leave one day as per one's Karma without prior notice to the victim, provided nothing extraordinary happens.

Knowledge is an endless process. We acquire knowledge through life experiences and also through our education systems. The object of education is learning and through this process we acquire knowledge in a particular field. To acknowledge this, one needs education. One can't explore anything without education. Education is a means of innovative ideas; by the ideas there is creativity; by the creativity there is development; and the development gives us a system of living in life. Education puts us at a level where we have the opportunity to choose our prospects for better living, that is, it puts us on a path of success, where we can have easy access to both society and spirituality. Education is a way by which we become capable of knowing our rights and duties toward our family, society and obviously the nation. Education provides us:

i. **Confidence**: Education puts us at such a knowledgeable level that we feel confident and comfortable at the workplace. Confidence is a tool of success and comes through education. It is the sense of surety of one's ability.

ii. **Competency**: Competency is the capability of the person to use the set of knowledge and skills appropriately to improve the performance of the job in question. Competencies are not skills but are understood as inherent qualities of an individual. Education supplemented competency, which proved to be a better performer. So, it is asserted that dedicated and devotional education puts one's self in such a firm state that it ensures success in every field.

iii. **Structure**. Education adds structure to one's life; right from waking up to sleeping, one has a set routine. It encourages one to make a schedule of activities that help one to excel in life.

iv. **Knowledge**, that'll last a lifetime: Education is not only a part of our lives, but it makes us so knowledgeable that it becomes useful for the rest of our lives. In this materialistic world, we are observing that there are drastic changes in all aspects and it is also asserted that there is no subject that will last for a lifetime. The lone entity that we think will survive for a lifetime is the learning skill, for which the base is education. We get knowledge through education and the knowledge gets strength through its uses and means. It is asserted that humans have such a quality that the individual remains learning (one's favorite skill) throughout his life as one has a passion for that, which lasts a lifetime (one can write one's current skill, such as "honesty is the best policy," knowledge to act honestly remains present in the individual's lifetime). When we make a connection with something, it leads us to learn, keeps us to remember all times, adds to our experiences and puts us in a position to improve.

v. **Quality of Life**. If one is healthy, wealthy and wise, the individual is considered to be living a quality of life. To sum up all these, it is quality education that puts one's life to this level, that is, to live a quality life. We have to remain vigilant at every distress action, as we have created the system of our life's activities such that both good and evil happen. We must keep our patience to face both, as both are emotional events. It is to be noted that it happens with all living organisms as it is the reward of our Karma given by the Almighty where all doubts of why happened to be at end. Secondly, these are the terms that run the life.

Education puts one's mind to work to conceive good thoughts and ideas, that is, sincere duty, being rational, being moralist, etc. It makes our lives fearless, tense-free and a free; it fosters a helping attitude toward the deserving; it creates a polluted, free environment. The teacher teaches the student to become educated, but when the student becomes experienced in a subject in which one gets education, the student becomes knowledgeable. So, knowledge is education and experience.

Knowledge has a beginning but no end. It becomes necessary to take action to know the power of education. An action means physical evidence, which our eyes can see very well. Anyone's action can give a sense of one's knowledge. So, it is the knowledge of a person through which one acts rationally and analytically that gives one's a quality life. Ethics as a way of life is concerned with the living of the human in this materialistic world where ethics are going to be absolute. In such a scenario, expressing our devotions to God by performing His duties shows our faith in the literature of ethics, which sustains healthy living. It means we step into His role by keeping ourselves in good conduct, living selflessly and performing our actions as an offering without desiring their fruits.

Ethics guides us at every step of our actions, which deeply influence our thinking, behavior and attitude toward ourselves, others and the universe. Ethics and our lifestyle or way of living are both inseparable; both complement each other; both exist because they are interrelated; and both would lose their meaning and significance without each other. Ethics as a way of life serves as the foundation of our character and behavior; it is the inseparable source of knowledge that has inspiration, guidance, philosophy and righteous conduct. This world is one family and we set up in their sub-families or groups as per their convenience at different places in the world with defined boundaries. We designate these as countries. Every country has its own constitution, culture and credit score, which differentiates these from one another. This credit score shows us the status of peace and prosperity in that country, which is an indicator of the position of the law in that state, that is, the status of prevailing ethics, thus showing which place is better for living, that is, whether God's norms for living are prevailing there or not.

Ultimately, we must live with nature; we must use biodegradable resources to maintain the ecological system of nature which makes our lives balanced and comfortable. Human beings who have adopted ethics as our way of life are completely responsible for our actions and the ways we choose to lead our lives. This means we follow our inherent nature and explore our inner beings to arrive at the absolute truth about ourselves and our existence. It cautions against the illusory nature of our existence and the evils that are hidden in it and suggests several ways and means to deal with it. It gives us complete freedom and living with a great sense of responsibility is our foremost duty. The primary and essential responsibility for maintaining nature and following the norms is our basic duty that comes with our position, status, knowledge and relationships. One has to perform these duties, as per one's position and status in life, with sincerity and selflessness. Every human being who is an aspect of God has to live, practice and protect his moral laws and if one does not follow or protect these laws, one is not entitled to Moksha, or salvation. Moksha is the highest reward, that is, free from death and birth scenarios. Therefore, each individual has to obey certain duties and obligations toward himself, one's family, one's ancestors, gods, other humans and other living beings to maintain the purpose of life. We have a primary duty to serve God and nourish Him because God keeps a protective watch over us and helps us secure our name, fame, wealth, progeny and other material comforts. The God exists not only outside in the macrocosm but also in the microcosm of each being as our internal organs and power centers. In their subtle states, they are the spiritual energies that reside in us and help us progress toward Aditi, the light and attain "Soma", the state of divine bliss. Therefore, when we nourish God, we also nourish ourselves and keep our bodies strong with the predominance of

Sattva. They are obliged to help us if we follow certain rules and restraints and perform rituals and spiritual sacrifices according to the Vedas. We must revere and respect the Vedas, because it is supposed to be revealed by God for the welfare and guidance of the world and contain nothing but truth. The Vedic texts do not favor rigid social structures. They suggest that one should follow the law according to one's discernment. Since discernment depends upon knowledge, intelligence and mental clarity, one should cultivate both physical and mental purity (Sattva). Life has five major purposes for a human being:

1. **Acquire Sufficient Knowledge**. The question is whether humans have reached the limit of knowledge or not. The answer is no, as our universe is so big that we are still unable to solve its mystery, such as which vast majority of material the universe is made up of. No one has an exact answer to this. So, knowledge is unending; acquire as much as you can, which will bring us peace and prosperity.
2. **Earn money to run the family without Malpractice**. Our earnings should be free from any misappropriations; that is, our earnings must be our hard-earned money and may not be addicted to any unfair means. It puts us to our duty with sincerity and keeps us well satisfied with the earnings we earn.
3. **Your service to the world**. It is our prime duty to take care of the world by adopting such measures that may not disturb the ecology system of the environment, whereas we are observing disturbances in the system, such as that in some regions there are huge rains damaging crops and inhabitancy and in adjoining a huge drought witness to happened, it also becomes the cause of damages to the crops, resulting in affecting the inhabitancy. It is also being observed that a huge fire has taken place due to the

extensive heat of the sun. It shows that the imbalance in the environment has taken place. It gets understood that we are the creators of all this as we have become a selfish entity, that is, a self-centered one, not caring for others and polluting the environment by emitting poisonous gases from heavy industry, which is due to more production than the prescribed limits. This gets the ecology system disturbed, creating an imbalance in nature. As a result, caring for the world becomes our primary responsibility and it is written in our ancient scriptures that humans have a responsibility to protect nature. In this context, our actions must be such that they do not disturb the ecological system of nature, so that life can be sustained on this planet.

4. **To fulfill someone's need for happiness**. It is the quality of a human being that we wish for all to be happy, but we observe that in the life of a human, both happiness and sorrow come side by side, we can get someone's sorrow less by sharing its sorrow; it can bring happiness to one's by fulfilling the needs that one deserves. It is also a fact that the donor feels happier in doing such acts, as humans have a quality of benevolence that gives them satisfaction from the heart.

5. **Believe in God** and follow the path of self-realization to achieve salvation. In the physical world, expansions are life and contractions are death. Whatever we cease to expand, that ceases to live. If one wishes to expand, it means one wishes to love nature and when one ceases to love, it leads to death. This is the law of life. Therefore, we must love God for love's sake, so we must do our duty for duty's sake; we must work for work's sake without looking for any reward. Humans are such creatures who wish for all the best, it shows that humans have a real faith in God.

We are asking for ethical development; the question is, which one is considered to be ethical development, or what is ethical development? Development means that living and non-living things are placed in such a specified and useful way that the ecological system of nature may not be disturbed. A country's credit score depends on its development. Human resources are the biggest assets of the nation, so the nation who have developed as much as infrastructure in education, that is, which have means where everyone has access to educational institutions and comfortable reading facilities, is considered to be a developed nation. Knowledge is power and education empowers it. It is not only empowering people to see the welfare of the deprived, but it is also a step toward human development. Education can be seen as both an objective and a component of development. As an objective, firstly, it is for the raising of human capabilities to pace with society and to achieve sustainable development and secondly, for economic growth, that is, education is essential for such acts. Education changes the life of man, that is, man into a human being and gets one upgraded to the capability of choosing the best alternative available. Thus, it enables us to adopt an appropriate adjustment method that may prove to be good in different situations and environments within a specified norm. So, education in every sense is one of the fundamental factors of development. Development needs substantial investment in human capital; the human capital theory postulates that the most efficient path to national development lies in the improvement of a country's population. It is education and training that can improve the population of a country and play a crucial role in the improvement of the productive capacity of the population. The living standard and work culture are indicators of the country's population density and development. Human resources are the ultimate basis of the wealth of a nation. It is the human being who, with his activeness, accumulates capital, exploits natural resources and gives a new shape to the country's economy.

It is human resources that bring rationality to socialism, nationalism, the political system and national development. It is human resources that eradicate poverty by putting people to use their skills and knowledge as per their convenience. There is a direct relationship between education and socio-economic development; it takes the nation to new economic heights. Education is responsible for changing human behavior, introducing rationalism into the environment and establishing the concepts of equality and impartiality. It gets governed by certain laws, powers and systems that are beyond mere political and sociological thinking and these cannot be exhausted by politics and sociology. Science, which is everywhere in our daily lives, has tried to lift this concept by applying ethical standards, which proved to be successful.

CHAPTER - 5

Uniqueness

What makes humans unique is that, they are the only ones who have the potential to reach near the Almighty God and sometimes do such heinous acts that humanity gets ashamed. So, it is understood that in all aspects, a human can go to such an extreme state where no other creature can dare to move for such an act; it makes humans unique. We must take the rational side, as rationalism makes one enthusiastic for virtuous acts. Whenever one does a work, an involvement of ethics comes into existence. So, ethics have their own unique role in every act; it is the role of moral development, which, in the present scenario, has become a basic necessity to bring awareness to humans about morality. It is asserted that our parents start teaching us about the good and bad right from childhood to maturity, keeping aside our careers and living standards. This makes sense because our ancestors paid attention to the rights, as rights stand for good and wrong for bad. It is to be noted that we were introduced to the concept of right and wrong at a very early age; even though our schooling has not started, it reflects the value of our culture that our ancestors were detrimental to doing the right work. The difference between good and bad has been so deeply absorbed in our genes that we pay high regard to such norms, make them a part of life and accept them as simple common sense. In schools, the students also study moral development, which enriches them in morality. They take morality as an asset in their lives, as it is the morality that decides their future. Such acts make humans unique. Humans have an extraordinary brain, though it is not big as compared to the body mass or as compared with other creatures in context to their structures. The human brain weighs only 3 pounds when fully grown up, which is only 2.5 percent of their body weight. This gives us the capability of reasoning and thinking at our own accord, which no other has such capability, thus making humans unique. Ethics comprises two aspects. First, it is a set of norms that comprise the standards of right and wrong; rights refer to obligation, welfare of society, fairness, etc., whereas wrong refers to stealing, murder, assault, slander, fraud, etc. Ethical standards also include the right to life, the right to freedom and the right to privacy. Secondly, it reveals the study and development of ethical standards. The new laws are coming into force day by day, which shows a certain deviation from ethical norms. The duty of the institution is to study the new laws and ensure that the new laws that are being enforced are reasonable and well-based. The study adheres to many functions, such as to promote the aim of the study, the study must make one knowledgeable, ensuring the avoidance of willing error. Coordination among different disciplines, the higher study involves great cooperation and coordination among different disciplines and institutions to achieve the goals. The ethical standard promotes the coordination of collaborative works by which we get to understand the meaning of cooperation, efficiency in production and ideas of innovations. The public supports the study, which reveals that ethics makes one so capable that their actions may build confidence among people to the extent that the public shows interest in investing in them for the development of the subject under study. The study promotes more important morals and social values such as social responsibility, medical care, human rights, animal welfare, compliance with laws and public health and safety. Ethics refers to values, principles and purposes. Values indicate good things; they stand by the meaning of life and living; principles indicate right things; they make one capable of responding as per the circumstances; and purposes indicate our existence in the universe. The knowledge of all this indicates the existence and purpose of our lives. So, firstly, we simply have to be honest with ourselves. As a human, I may not be corrupt in any aspect. My human nature should keep me treating all the lives in this world with respect, that is, Vasudhaiva Kutumbakam (the world is one family). My human nature should keep me putting all my sincere efforts toward my job without worrying about the results, as one is purer and sincere. Keeping in view all these aspects, it has come to an understanding that humans do not worry for themselves but have a concept that everyone should be aware of right and wrong; hence, here prevails a right everywhere; such thoughts prevail in humans only, which makes humans unique.

CHAPTER - 6

Nature

The ultimate reality of nature, the question reveals which one is the complete entity; in other words, to whom we can call a complete one. Philosophers put forth their views to ascertain the version accordingly. In general, reality is viewed as "my reality may not be the reality of others," so it is taken as perception, beliefs and attitudes toward that reality in question. It indicates that there is little criticism over this issue, as perception and beliefs are the words of discussion. Ultimate reality is defined as the entity which has totality and supremacy in all the realities. In Western philosophy, reality has two different aspects: the nature of reality itself and the relationship between the mind and reality. In this context, philosophers view it as the reality being independent of perception and beliefs, so it is called realism. Philosophers assert that any object whose characteristics are not influenced by any human artifact can be given the name of realism of that object; we can also call it idealism, as ideas and reality come from the mind, which is a manifestation of God. In their views, reality is an idea of the mind that comes after thorough scrutiny. Some philosophers assert that we are living in a material world where we sense and feel the entity and put our remarks accordingly against that entity, keeping in view its philosophical and scientific aspects to ascertain the facts and justify our views toward that entity. This idea is generated in the mind, so the mind is the only cause to ascertain reality. The essence of this idea is that only the self is real and exists; the rest are all materials which we experience externally, which may be a dream or illusion. The philosophers also assert that even the universe is potentially a projection of one's mind. This idea is not recommended by some philosophers with the reason that reality cannot be verified independently, as here one's mind, consciousness and perception are the only factors to create reality, which is unjustifiable. Indian philosophers keep God as an ultimate reality and view it as: The Almighty has created our body and mind such that it has access to infinite knowledge, the knowledge that makes human beings to access the difference between the real and the unreal. It is asserted that in our daily life, a human exists in such a state when a human exists without a body and mind and this state is given the name of sleep.

There is one more state in our daily life when one thinks of one's intellect, one's reason, one's mind, one's emotions, one's tears from the eyes and to analyze this state is a difficult scenario. Humans also have a state, a state of deep sleep, that is, a state of absolute existence, a state beyond entity, but one's ability and memories go up in this state. To study this state, one needs to study it in the context of psychology or mentally, but this knowledge has proved to be inadequate for the purpose of knowing what status of a human being exists in this deep sleep state. The characteristics of the mind are that it only thinks of what is happening in front of it and it cannot know what is behind it. Secondly, the mind does not work in sleep. This inability of the mind shows that a human being has no knowledge of oneself. It is very strange and mysterious that a human being knows everything about others but does not know oneself. We have means of knowing others, but we have no means of knowing ourselves. Why? Because the mind has no knowledge of its own source. It means in deep sleep, one existed but cannot know in what condition one existed, as there is no means of knowing the condition of one's existence in the deep sleep state. Therefore, there is a peculiar way of knowing this knowledge other than mental knowledge. Psychological knowledge also does not hold good here, as it involves the activity of the senses, which is the job of the mind, whereas the mind remains inactive in this state. Another way of knowing ourselves is the way of self-assertiveness, indubitable feelings, which one calls a realization. One has a realization of oneself and one is here for certain reasons, the effects of which others feel accordingly. This shows that reality does not need any proof to ascertain and is self-evident. It is also observed that one feels happier, joyful and tireless after awakening than after a day's work. This is so because a human being has so many interactions with people of different ideologies and natures at work. This may give him knowledge, experience, enjoyment and all of this becomes possible with the activity of one's mind and body, whereas one's mind and body are inactive in sleep, which becomes a cause of happiness.

So, it becomes certain that one exists wholly in deep sleep. It is also observed that one feels more than one's appearance, that is, one has a transcendent approach that makes one conscious of one's mental attitudes. One is not simply a human being; one is a pure being and has an association with only pure consciousness. This being is the state of one's deep sleep associated with consciousness and a remembrance of the past to our existence, which is in the deep sleep stage. To recall a memory means recalling a past experience and a past experience means awareness of that event. This shows that one is pure and conscious of self at every stage and nothing more, nothing less. This also shows that one is ultimately real and not unreal. This is the activity in life that one seeks in fulfilling desires and aspirations. One's struggle in life to seek purity and consciousness, even when one sometimes makes violations contrary to purity, one's conscience makes them awake to do what is right. The characteristic of a human being is not to sit idly but to work until it ends. This makes a human being infinite, having no limits of any sort. So, there is an ultimately real something and to whom we can call the ultimately real, which is a pure being, consciousness and one and only one, which is immanent and, at the same time, transcendent. The state of being everywhere, in everything, in every form, in every condition, is called immanence. All these properties pertain to the one and the only one, that is, God. Therefore, God is the ultimate reality of nature.

The existence and nature of consciousness, consciousness is a sense of one's actions. It is a natural, subtle phenomenon, not a physical object to be considered. Consciousness is simply the awakening of a human being to being conscious of any event occurring in the environment in which we live. Life is full of events and how we make these events successful depends on our consciousness, to which we must act appropriately. So, becoming conscious becomes a matter of study for which philosophers put forth their views accordingly.

Before we delve into the modern philosophers, the ancient Indian philosophers (Rishis) studied the concept of consciousness and we find a vast literature available in the Rig Vedas. Consciousness is an entity that relates to the nature of the self. Sometimes, a human being may suffer a head injury, resulting in the loss of memory and consciousness, but the person remains alive. This shows that consciousness is associated with the activity of the body and cannot be measured analytically but can be measured physically. According to Vedic scriptures, there are two types of consciousness that exist not only in humans but in all creations. One is pure consciousness and the second is ego consciousness.

Pure consciousness is universal, passive, eternal, individual and pure. Its source is God himself and gives rise to soul consciousness, termed as pure consciousness. Ego consciousness is considered as qualities, dualities, modifications and dynamism. Its source is nature in its dynamism and differentiated state. The word ego stands for "I am" and becomes active due to self-activity. This ego is also an aspect of nature, so we may call it ego consciousness and in Vedic scripture, it is named "chitta," which means whole body and mind consciousness. "The activity of the brain is mind; the activity of the mind is intellect and the activity of the intellect is chitta. This is such an activity when a human has full concentration on the task at hand." This consciousness brings about an awakening in humans, resulting in dynamism in human nature, so we may call this dynamism consciousness or ego consciousness. This forms the basis of ego consciousness.

It is understood that human beings have a potency of higher consciousness, which is due to the composition of human beings as follows:

i. The senses (eye, ear, nose, tongue and skin); these are the integral parts of our lives and give us the senses of sight, hear, smell, taste and touch, respectively, which aid us in survival, development, learning and adaptation of humans and animals.

ii. The lower mind (the manas); from the top to the bottom of the body, there are manas, koshas, or cells; every cell in the body is accompanied by memory and intelligence, not just of this life but of millions of years; it does not have intellect, which is only with the brain.

iii. The self-sense (ego), when the whole body and mind are devoted to certain activities and acclaimed by themselves, is called the ego.

iv. The higher mind, or intelligence (budhi), is that which is capable of discerning the difference between truth and falsehood.

All these acts form the basis for the ego consciousness that a human requires to undergo ego consciousness. Humans have the potency to act on these in a strength of one, which results in the formation of numerous ideas and relationships with the consciousness and makes us ready for limitless actions. In this context, our old scripture gives the definitions of the ordinary mind and the distinguishing mind. The ordinary mind is considered merely a receptacle of thoughts, feelings, etc. that one receives from the external environment. Each thought has a universal meaning that enters the human consciousness as per the person's potency of receptivity and state of mind. Thus, the ordinary mind is merely a receptacle of thought but not a creator of ideas; it is only the recipient of existing thoughts from the external environment and stores them as its own. The intelligent mind, or higher mind, is taken as responsible for thinking, reasoning and discerning. It takes one to go deep into the matter, which solves the problem and enlightens one about the external environment. It is believed that the nature of consciousness is a projection of an intelligent mind and intelligent mind is nature's gift considering consciousness is also nature's gift to human beings, more or less this may be.

Consciousness and existence Consciousness is a reality and a subject in the process of cognition and can be understood only by the self. Depending on how one observes it, making it a part of life and maintaining it in life is a crucial task for human beings. However, to know all these, one has to go beyond the mind and learn to look at the mind with detachment and dispassion. Detachment and dispassion make one independent from this materialistic world; in Sanskrit, it is called "vairagya" to live without craving. It is through detachment that one is able to free one's consciousness from the clichés of unknowledgeable actions. Discarding responsibility and relationships does not give rise to detachment, but to understand the need for dispassion is more important than to actualize its wisdom in real and personalized circumstances. According to the scripture, it is possible to transfer one's consciousness to others and from one source to another through a spiritual process. This shows that consciousness can exist in the living stage of a human being and some memories one can retain even after death. It is also possible to transfer consciousness to others theoretically through teaching, communication, etc., which may be effective or not. According to scripture, the universal consciousness, or pure consciousness, or the center of human consciousness is the innermost reality, as it exists in all beings; it is considered eternal, which means existing, so its existence or non-existence does not require any proof, as Veda versions are understood to be a true one.

CHAPTER - 7

Meaning of Life

What constitutes a good and fulfilling life? Firstly, let's consider the necessity of human beings in this universe. According to the Vedas, which are a treasury of knowledge, they explain the function of human beings on this planet. Human beings are meant to assist God in maintaining social, moral and physical order by implementing the cosmic law of nature, known as "Rta." Rta stands for "divine law or truth," the divine law that governs all life and comprises virtues, ethics and philosophy. It is a law that holds true for everyone.

Everyone aspires to live their best life, but it gets vary from person to person, as everyone has their own feelings and thoughts. However, the good and fulfilling life is that which is liked by all and brings pleasure to all, is considered a truthful life. The path that constitutes righteous acts leads one to a life that is regarded as good and fulfilling. Fulfillment means attaining a state of satisfaction, which should be the aim of everyone's life.

We are living in a materialistic world where one has to interact with many people of varying temperaments while working to earn a living. So, one has to overcome all these by adopting healthy conduct and behavior; it keeps one satisfied and helps one to achieve the goals. Nature has provided us with a fascinating environment in which adequate water, adequate forests and sufficient land are available for actions and interactions.

These three things are the fundamental requirements of living and we call this an ecology system, the system that gives life to all creatures. To save the system from deterioration, the only way is to maintain the balance between nature and humans, which is by taking appropriate land use, conserving forests and making appropriate use of water; otherwise, life will be in trouble. So, first and foremost, one's assistance to God is that one should save nature by indulging himself in right practice. This way, one can make one's life a valuable one. Life is not only limited to food, clothes and shelter; one also needs a lot of extra to keep pace with society. So, to accomplish these needs, one has to work more, as desires have put the human in an imbalanced position, thus forcing one's to work more, which leads to health hazards. So, to avoid this, if one works quietly cautiously and one's decisions are based on logic, one can minimize desires, which leads one's to a good and fulfilling life.

The following are some principles that, if followed, can lead to a sense of satisfaction and fulfillment:

1. **Time**. Time is a crucial factor and it doesn't wait for anyone. Therefore, utilizing time must be a top priority for humans to succeed in any endeavor. It's time that fosters punctuality and sets life's goals. Life itself is a challenge and by managing time effectively, one can feel satisfied and fulfilled. The quality of human life is measured by the quality of time used for productive purposes. Thus, time should be a priority in life and time spent on unnecessary conversations (time-wasting) should be minimized.
2. **Discipline in Life**. We need works for earnings, which are required to run an ordered life and it is asserted that to run an ordered life, we have to follow the discipline. So, discipline is the learning orders or instructions of a particular area, necessitated for the self-actualization, personal growth of an individual and in view of maintaining and enhancing

social productivity. All these are required to run a tense-free life, which we can only maintain by following the path of discipline. So, following discipline in life is as important as meals are for survival, so discipline is important to lead an ordered life. It reflects a sense of good conduct, so it is considered a key to success for any venture. Discipline should be first on himself so that it inspires others to become such ideals. So, making discipline a part of life gives one a sense of goodness and happiness. It is asserted that the habit of discipline comes to us from our parents; it is its real source; it is our hereditary.

3. **Accountable Life**. Accountability means living with integrity, that is, one is accountable to his words, thoughts and actions, which means fully owing to everything that happens in one's life. It empowers one's to be an authority, such as one of ownership, which gives one's a sense of his status, where one's stand in context to the assignment for which one has held accountable, as accountability is not sustainable without authority. It allows one to seek solutions to the best for sustainable success. It is accountability that puts all the concern into acting as one, which keeps the team on the right track. Accountability is not about perfection, as it may sometimes not reach our desired results, but it always proves to be fit as per our desires, which adds to our personal values. It also improves the efficiency of the project as accountability keeps one on course till one fulfills the commitment as desired.

4. **Forgiveness** is the quality in humans that gives one's sense of goodness and in the context of humanity, it is considered a benevolence. It is a very big asset in humans that one possesses such thoughts, that is, to forgive others for their errors. It is considered a strong man in all aspects. In addition to this, the forgiver has the blessings of others too, which keeps him happy in life and a feeling

of satisfaction is also liberating in a human being. Both forgiveness and revenge are acts of human nature to solve problems; they may vary as per time and situation. It is understood that there may be more forgivers by whom a beautiful and peaceful life has happened, so forgiveness is treated as divine. One must adopt this quality first for himself.

5. **Purpose of Life**. It is very tedious and complex to answer this and I think it is beyond the approach of a human. So, it is up to us to find out the purpose of life. In my view, we are here because of the gift of nature, so taking care of nature is the purpose of our life and this is also as per Vedic studies. Firstly, we have to understand that, what is life? A human body with a soul constitutes a life; there is no life without a soul; breathing makes the soul to operate; when there is no breathing, the soul comes out of the body in subtle form and moves to the cosmos; it is said that death has occurred. In Vedic philosophy, there is no death; there is birth and rebirth; that is, the soul that has left the body has entered into some other womb to take birth. So, there is life after life; the soul, which keeps the man alive, is the creation of God, has no form and never dies; it is eternal, remains active in the living body as long as man remains active and leaves the body when one's get old, his capability of activeness gets exhausted and death is said to occur. The soul moves to his native place from where it has come, that is, to the God, that is, the pure soul, which moves as per the Karma of that soul. If one has proved to be an ideal, then the God gets that soul absorbed in Himself, to whom we call salvation, that is, that soul gets freed from the birth and death cycle. Rest all we have to take birth and rebirth. The purpose of our lives is to protect nature. Nature has given us the five basic elements, that is, air, water, earth, fire and sky, of which

the human body is composed. Therefore, to take care of these five basic elements, which we can make possible by optimum use of air, optimum use of water, optimum use of land and optimum use of fire, it will make our sky clear, it will keep humans free and we will come to the conclusion that to save nature means to save the life of humans. In my view, it must be the purpose of life.

6. **Enhancement in Life** means augmenting or adding value in life. It is asserted that we used to enhance something in life that moved our lives and generally we consider it our success; it brings happiness into our lives. So, it becomes an important tool for human beings who have the quality and potency of learning and strive to learn throughout their lives. Enhancement may be subjective or objective; subjective is when one augments himself for his favorite subject, that is, the subject that one thinks is more important for him, such as having a luxurious car in life, which may be life-enhancing for someone. Certain things that have a common objective, that is, benefiting the masses, come under the category of objective enhancement, such as "honesty is the best policy". To get augments for this subject makes the masses a violation-free society, which is the need of the day. Such enhancement in life gives satisfaction and happiness in one's life, so one must have the characteristic of enhancing himself in good aspects; it encourages dynamism, which is a life.

7. **Be an Ideal**. An ideal means one is the best suitable in all aspects; this then happens when one's action speaks louder than words and this then happens when others quote the example of one's action. It happens when one remains in discipline; discipline makes the man perfect, but the ideal is perfect at its own will. So, it is difficult to define an ideal, as in this intellectual world, everybody is an ideal of someone and at the end, we come to the

conclusion that we are all an ideal of the Vedas, whose literature is eternal, best suitable and enforceable in all aspects and has not been claimed by anyone. In my view, the ideal person is one who has the qualities of honesty. Honesty is such a quality in a human being that it acts as impartial and sincere, so it is liked by all castes and creeds. Responsibility, or being responsible, is also one of the best qualities in a human being. Due to mistakes, the quality of a responsible person is to work willingly and freely. Responsibility makes a person accept challenges and commitments. Cooperation inspires us to work jointly as what we can achieve jointly is not possible to achieve separately; the demerit is only one; our credit gets divided whereas merits are unlimited; such as, common objectives are only solved by cooperation; it provides us unity and harmony to achieve optimum results, etc. So, an ideal man must be cooperative.

8. **Chasing your beliefs** or how to believe in ourselves is a concept of mind associated with the purpose of life and must be chased. It justifies one's knowledge and talent, adds value to our lives and brings fulfillment to them. This fulfillment covers all that we require in our lives and the truth is that we still lack by our self-confidence. On one hand, it is the belief that fulfills our desires and on the other hand, we have self-doubt in building our self-confidence, which is a source of misery for humans. Everything that we have in our lives is the result of our beliefs, so to build beliefs in ourselves means to build confidence in ourselves. It took one's to chase the beliefs, if the following steps were taken into consideration, one will be amazed to see the results.

   i. **Believe it's possible**. It is believed that we have the potential to achieve success in any task, whatever others say or whatever state we are in. Our concentration must be on our task and its accomplishment.

ii. **Visualize it**. Think about what our status would be if we had already achieved the task.

iii. **Act as if**. Always choose the path that leads to the completion of the task.

iv. **Take action toward our goals**. Make sure that we are the competent ones to take action and any fear cannot stop it; nothing happens in life without performing actions.

9. Consider duty bigger than ourself; putting duty more than ourselves represents the good characteristics of the human being. Duty means actions, the actions that decide the future of a human being, resulting in one's happiness and sorrow. Right actions put one into happiness and wrong actions put one into trouble. So, doing the right thing gives one a sense of happiness and satisfaction. Therefore, duty that gives benefits to the masses is a bigger duty, such as our great leaders who freed India from the clutches of the British; that is, they dedicate their duty to the nation where the masses get change in their lives; this is a bigger duty than themselves. Then there is the global warming issue, which our India has taken up with global leaders as the whole universe is being affected. India has been recognized as the champion of the earth, so such duties are considered a bigger duty as the masses will get the benefit of such acts.

The difference between conviction, belief and knowledge A conviction is a firm belief that one has on a specific matter. It is a serious term generally used in legal matters. It is different from beliefs; belief is considered the truth; it is subject to change, whereas conviction is the firm truth; it is based on the facts by which conviction is being created. A conviction is a declaration made by the authority that one is found guilty of a criminal offense. The conviction is such a status to a human that one feels himself different from the rest of the world; that is, one feels himself an inferior one, a nominated bad one.

Belief is that one, which one consider to be a truth? Everyone has their own beliefs; some say honesty is the best policy; some say even philosopher Chanakya says honest people are the first who face hardship, giving the example that straight trees are cut first. So, belief is there because it is based on one's experience and background and is subject to change. Knowledge, is a justified fact that one acquires through people, experience and education, is a medium to complete the process of acquisition.

i. Importance of knowledge.

   a. It makes one aware of right and wrong.
   b. It is more powerful than a sword.
   c. It is a lifesaving medicine in case of any mishap.
   d. It is behind the success of a person.
   e. It makes one honorable too.

ii. Characteristics of knowledge.

   a. It has no boundaries.
   b. It never decays.
   c. Facts and values are the basis of knowledge.
   d. A miracle; it goes on increasing, as much as one goes on distributing.
   e. Knowledge is a vocation.

In conclusion, conviction is not used for good people, but it is true and based on facts. Beliefs were once considered true, but they are subject to change. Knowledge, to know anything, requires knowledge, which we get through education, experiences, etc. and is necessary to run a life. Therefore, there is no life without knowledge.

Part 2

Conscience

CHAPTER - 1

Meaning

It is asserted that if we observe something complex and that too understandable, that is, the universe, which is so esteemed that it has no limits, means infinite. It is a composition of matter and energy. The human, who himself is complex and understandable, is also a composition of matter and energy, that is, earth, water, air, fire and sky, having the potency to absorb himself in this universe and keeping one's status at the highest among all the creatures. It is asserted that this wonderful human is a creation of omnipotent God, though God is invisible, but we feel sense of that by observing this foolproof process of the solar system functioning tirelessly without any interruption, that is, a time-bound system comprising 365 days forming a year that further gets split into seasons, that is, spring, summer, rainy and winter. In the same way, humans, whose functions have been pre-defined, work tirelessly around the clock, which is controlled by a subtle energy that we all call it "the soul", which exists in the body. As per our scripture, it is God's element, as this is also invisible but potent, without which one cannot have life, so it is asserted that humans are an element of God. A human who is equipped with such wonderful resources that it put one in such suspense that even without asking the question of the subject to the conscience, how does the answer get developed in the conscience of the human being? One thinks it a mystery, but it happens. In Hindi, it is also called "Antar *Atma.*" This does not exist as any organ of the body but exists in the body in subtle form; it makes the human aware of any wrongful activity being carried out or even thinks so. It is also to be said that it is one's hereditary as it indicates the knowledge of our ancestors, thereby making us feel happy doing the right action. This is due to the fact that our ancestors always accepted right actions and right action is that action, that is, in favor of all. The conscience, which resides in a human's body and possesses all valid knowledge, is understood to be acquired through inheritance or other means such as knowledge gained in schools, colleges, etc. It gives strength to the conscience and remains active in all human's actions to guide one's to do the right actions. It is also understood that it is a self-knowledge, the knowledge that one feels is a part of one's life, though it is treated as hereditary knowledge. Humans consider this a self-knowledge. It is also a fact that one is known by one's hereditary. If we go through our past culture of living, it was absolutely righteous, which get flow in our genes, a biological fact that we observe in small children even when no one teaches them, but acting righteous means the effects of our hereditary, as our ancestors always had right thinking, which put us on the right path. On the other hand, conscience is treated as God's voice, so the study of this complex one, that is, conscience, to get it understood becomes imperative for us and seems to be an interesting one.

Conscience is inbuilt in the body of a human being at the core of one's heart, confirming one's own sense of right and wrong; it is just gut instinct. It is as such that one feels good about doing good work and feels guilty about doing some immoral work. It is the human spice that thinks so fairly, that this quality makes humans distinct creatures and puts them at the apex of other creatures. Secondly, humans are cooperative and wish to work in groups where one gets an opportunity to understand the nature of others and feels comfort and pleasure if the ideas of similarity exist and if they do not tally, even then it is possible to get that work done without any interruption. This includes the human as a quality, that is, “a conscious creature,” which keeps him fit to live in a civilized society and ultimately such societies take the shape of villages, towns, cities, etc. and at the end, this leads us to a political organization that defines the way of living in context to socially, politically and economically. It is God’s gift to human beings that it puts a silent alarm on one’s to get one’s awareness of his every act of undertaking. It is an initial guide that warns us when we are not obeying God’s norms, that is, when we harm others for our own self-interest. Conscience is the most fundamental of all moral duties. Conscience, which is invisible, makes itself visible by its action; the action that proved to be correct keeps the sanctity of the identity and an authentic one. This makes one capable of controlling, monitoring, evaluating and executing one’s every action to safeguard the individual from violations and to follow standard, defined norms, which makes one an ideal human. It is asserted that conscience is the degree of integrity and honesty of each human being because it has proven to be a virtue. It is the degree to which one focuses on one objective at a time, that is, the objective of absolute good or absolute right. One can’t reach the absolute, but one can come closer to the absolute, which depends on the quality of one’s conscience. Unfortunately, this relative approach to the truth in one’s life changes as per the prevailing situations; this is the instinctual nature of the human that one has acquired from their heritage and environment. Moral conscience is in one’s heart and makes him available at the appropriate moments to do good and to avoid evil. It bears witness to the authority of truth, that is, God, who has created the human being and human beings who have welcomed its commandments. It is up to one’s will to act according to the conscience or to act at any particular moment; it is the freedom of choice that exists in a human being and may be utilized appropriately. It means that one takes decisions and actions in accordance with the dictums of the individual's conscience; this leads to an evolution and refinement of the conscience and puts one in inner peace of mind. Conscience claims universal authority, which one can narrate in theistic terms but cannot depend on other entities as it has its own existence and sanctity. A conscious person's conscience is always upright and truthful and they take decisions according to reason. If one acts against one's own conscience, this leads to an involution and the feeling of a troubled conscience being observed. If any of the basic functional organs of the one gets injured by accident or suffers due to illness, it is observed that awareness of the one being suffered. In such a case, conscience no longer functions, leading us to the conclusion that the overall functional ability of the brain leads to decisions and actions. It has a unique character due to its infinite complexity; it is integrated (if a part of the body collapses, the whole system may suffer or collapse) and it is continuously changing its decision (new information is constantly absorbed, affecting and differentiating levels of conscience). The brain has a hierarchical nature and capacity to make final and meaningful decisions. It is responsible for whether one decides to commit himself to rationalism and truth, as philosophers and scientists do for their jobs, or to deceive others, as do criminals.

In this way, conscience formulates every aspect of life, from the lowest to the highest, even to the transcendental and sublime. These transcendental qualities exist in those people who are spiritual, can understand and realize the incoming information and thus make decisions and actions in seconds. Such persons possess a high level of conscience and usually have a high vision, a vision that can inspire others and aim to always help others. It is such a vision that a new quality of conscience eventually emerges to sacrifice self-interest for the common cause.

Sacrificing self-interest leads to a higher level of conscience, which is a tough task as one has to put the common good above self-interest. This then happens when one is deterministic about the task and one whose passions are to pursue the search for truth or those who sacrifice their lives for the societies in which they live. It is observed that such actions provide relief and gaiety to societies and make the public feel rejuvenated and in better health. These decisions depend on this individual state of conscience, whether it may act as destructive or constructive, affecting sometimes the whole nation. On the other hand, there is low conscience, which allows one to deceive people for their own self-interest; their actions may also affect the nation. This shows the quality of the leadership and the level of conscience. This high and low conscience is due to the education that our conscience has received; it means if our conscience is not well educated, that is, our conscience is not well formed and is not well-equipped to analyze right from wrong. So, it is our duty to align our conscience with the truth so that whenever we come across any problem, our conscience guides us well. One has the right to act according to conscience and in freedom so that one can take decisions as per his own wisdom. One can't be forced to act contrary to conscience, nor can one be prevented from acting according to one's conscience. Human personality consists of intellect, emotions and willpower; these attributes help the individual to take decisions. The knowledge of making these decisions is called wisdom; it is the intelligence in one's mind to understand and perceive the world around them. To attain wisdom is a lifelong process and if it is achieved through spirituality, it leads one to an ultimate life. Wisdom is the power that enables us to exercise knowledge, experience, intellect, common sense and perceptiveness at an appropriate time. It is observed that wisdom and knowledge are the hard work of an individual, but it is evident that besides hard work, it is not possible to have wisdom and knowledge without the knowledge of spirituality. It is understood that wisdom and knowledge are only obtained by the grace of God. The education of conscience is indispensable for human beings, as human beings very easily come into the influence of the negative concept, as negative shines more than positive and one gets indulged in sin by preferring their own decisions and rejecting the authoritative teachings. This shows the incompleteness of one's behavior, that is, education without reasons. Education of the conscience is a lifelong venture; in childhood, it awakens the child to the inner knowledge recognized by the conscience and in the adult stage, it teaches virtue. It prevents one from experiencing fear, selfishness, pride and anxiety, which are caused by guilt and feelings of complacency that come out of one's weaknesses and faults. The formation of a good and pure conscience is the work of education, training, practice and experience, which makes one to be ever more human and leads one over more fully to the truth, putting one in respect for life and making one fit in interpersonal relationships. Pure conscience means a pure and sincere heart; it means one's life is guided by the objective standards of moral conduct, which is the ultimate aim of life. Education is long, but our lives are short, so there is no end to education; life has to pass through different stages in which one has to pass through different and complex problems that require deeper and better application of education, which is only possible through education, which makes the difference between virtue and vice. Human virtues are firm attitudes, stable disposal and governing one's action according to reasons and faith. Sometimes one gets confused with the prevailing situation and is helpless in making a decision. In such cases, one must always seek what is right and good based on one's experience and consciousness and act as per the divine laws; it takes one to the right decision. The one's conscience gets increased over time by indulging in and solving out the varying acts by taking decisions of right, which get enhanced by attending the seminars on ethics delivered by eminent scholars and also by saints. This gives one a well-rounded understanding of one's values and principles, helps one, get judged whether one's action is right or wrong and also indicates how much one is ethical in one's character and behavior. So, conscience is such a subtle element that is loyal to ethics.

Conscience refers to two functions, that is, what a person believes is right and how a person decides what is right. It means the role of awareness and the role of decision-making act simultaneously, which recognizes the strength of conscience. Awareness shows one's ethical capability in values and principles, which one gains through education, experience and decision-making and one's ethical capability in one's actions, which one gains by keeping himself aware of facts and evidence. This keeps one evaluating the situation as per the circumstances. The conscience, which is well versed in both the activities and nature, keeps us to know ourselves and our environment and puts us to act accordingly. It shows that conscience makes us well aware of our deeply held moral principles and motivates us to act upon these principles; this also helps us in assessing our character, our behavior and ultimately ourself against these principles. As such, conscience is taken as subjective in character as it has the suggestion of self only, an inward-looking, subtle matter; this reflects an etymological relation between the notion of conscience and that of consciousness. Whereas conscience and consciousness are two terms having different meanings, consciousness is related to awareness of the mind and conscience is a moral dimension. Philosophers had significant discussions on conscience and have come to the understanding that conscience is a form of moral self-awareness that possesses several qualities. Aquinas, a key thinker on conscience, describes the conscience as the application of knowledge to activity in a given situation. It raises the question, that where from this knowledge has comes.

The philosopher introduced a term for this, which we call "synderesis." Synderesis is not the same as conscience but an innate quality of the mind to apprehend the eternal laws. Two distinct views about the relationship between conscience and synderesis emerged: the first view stating a voluntaristic one, as the desire for the good is equated with emotional reactions when one follows evil instead of good. Second, is an intellectualistic view by Aquinas, who states that synderesis is an unerring intellectual dispositional potentiality that provides general truth to the conscience for a specific purpose. Bonaventure, a Franciscan thinker's view on synderesis and conscience, considers conscience a rational faculty that acts as per one's action and is well connected to the will and emotions of the one. On the other hand, they consider synderesis an effective one for the human being as it stimulates us to do good. Bonaventure divides the conscience into two parts. The first part is a very practical principle that is, the power of the truth, such as "obey God", "honor the parents" and "do not harm the neighbors." This is due to innate qualities and cannot be lost to any person, regardless of how bad one may be. The second part of conscience involves the application of very general principles to all situations and is also innate, but it can be mistaken due to misapplication of the first by ignorance or faulty reasons. Misapplication means the conscience, whose mission is always to do right, gets involved in the performance of evil actions. It is understood that conscience, whose actions are developed through experience and practical principles of behavior, lacks such content. So, generalizing on activities performed in accordance with the principle of synderesis, Bonaventure considers synderesis the "spark of conscience" and an effective one for human beings because synderesis is a drive for good. The philosopher considered that the formation of ethical rules by conscience is for the implementation of the human being's desire for the good and another aspect of the desire for good is that, humans naturally have a desire for the good. The philosopher did not consider conscience and synderesis as separate concepts, as they view conscience as driven by synderesis and, at the same time, view conscience as directing synderesis. This means that though conscience and synderesis are two concepts, the philosopher regards them as interpenetrating one another. For Thomas Aquinas, synderesis is never mistaken, as the first and general principles of the synderesis are to "do good and avoid evil" and "obey God," which are very helpful in human activities, whereas conscience has much more content, which is derived from experiences and instructions, by virtue of prudence, one calls these secondary principles. So, as per Aquinas, the function of conscience is to apply the general principle of synderesis and the secondary principle developed from prudence is to be applied in particular circumstances. Aquinas asserted that the knowledge that one has in his mind comes from the synderesis, which the philosopher considered a natural process of the human mind by which we apprehend without inquiry the basic principles of conduct that are helpful in human activities. Philosophers have the view that conscience makes a mistake due to its content, as it becomes erroneous by not applying the appropriate content at the appropriate time, which means failure of conscience is due to the content, which needs to be clearly thought through. For Aquinas, it is due to ignorance, which is of two types. Ignorance that can be overcome by applying one's reason (evincible ignorance) and ignorance that cannot be overcome by applying one's reason (invincible ignorance) Invincible ignorance is doing something wrong when one does not have knowledge of the content, whereas evincible ignorance is doing something wrong when one is capable of knowing better. Aquinas concludes that in spite of the innate knowledge of right and wrong that one has, one makes mistakes in applying this knowledge. Then it is our conscience that guides us and moves us to act. Actions can be wrong because ignorance, which could have been avoided (evincible), means our action is morally wrong. Mistakes come out of ignorant action that one could not have avoided (invincible), which means our actions are not morally wrong. The philosopher Scotus views conscience as having a much more dynamic role to play in the personality of a human being; they asserted that the development of virtue makes one toward the right to dictate, which develops a habit of one's to perform virtuous action. Scotus regards conscience as offering a way for right actions and an exercise for conscience that determines the proper actions from the principle of synderesis. Keeping this on track, one can perform actions that give a sense of the development of the relevant virtues. The role of conscience in such acts leads one to the habit of always thinking of virtues. Ideally, the moral virtues are unified, since a perfect virtuous person is one who possesses all virtues. In scout's view, the ideal virtuous person is one who possesses practical wisdom, such as Aristotle, whose skills determine what should be done in given circumstances.

CHAPTER - 2

Function

Function of the conscience, each of us, by any means, may have talked about our conscience; sometimes it might have pricked us and sometimes it might have "butted in" against our will and pinched us. It means our conscience is objecting to the actions we undertake, such as stealing. However, the nature of conscience is obscure and, on the other hand, it is a philosophical discussion taken as complex, as the entity is formless, but its senses are so effective that one has to accept its authenticity. The notion of conscience is very old, though it has not been called by conscience, as it is supposed to be God's voice and guidance. In the soul, conscience functions as thinking and emotions, whereas mind and heart function with acquaintance and convictions, with reasons. These three components work for the soul and determine the status of one's conduct and come to the conclusion of how much one functions as God's intent in their day-to-day life. The scripture shows that one is responsible for the matter used for the mind, heart and conscience and to the extent to which one develops and uses this as God's intent. This makes sense in how accurately one observes the environment and seeks expectations from others. In the soul, conscience functions as the repository of priorities: values, defaults, choices and the will, though all are spiritual phenomena, they are no less real for being such. It is observed that if one considers conscience a general entity, taking no care for it as generally one does, it means one has left the conscience in a vulnerable condition. This makes the conscience act not as per God's norms, but it acts by the materialistic and narcissistic agenda of the day. Such thinking puts conscience as just a place-marker and keeps one ignorant about the power of the conscience. Adopting the culture of conscience realizes the benefit of the power of conscience, which aids us in loving God and our neighborhood, an essential part of our life for sustainability. Conscience acts as an assistant to the soul, maintaining vigilance over one's thoughts and emotions and assisting the mind and the heart to work together to offer maximum benefit to the individual. Understanding conscience and caring accordingly puts one in realization of the power of faith working for one's life. We call it an action of the conscience, which puts the heart and mind into harmony or discord it and works for the soul in accordance with the prevailing situation. This is God's assistance (conscience) to human beings to keep the soul in proper working order and spiritually inscribe His Laws on the souls of human beings so that in every person, there exists a sense of righteousness, goodness and holiness. It is a fact that we all have more or less such senses, depending on our capability and how much we are serving as God's intends.

It is also a fact that the majority of people do not pay much attention to such senses of righteousness, goodness and holiness. But they have the notion in their minds that something is permissible and something is not, right is permissible and evil is not (as already explained). This shows that human beings are an image of God because right is always permissible by God and evil is always discarded–a universal truth. It means humans have a conscience and their conscience knows the difference between right and wrong and even holiness, which they use to make decisions of various sorts. However, these terms often have to be filtered through a selfish view of the world.

Conscience is a judgment of reasons by which one perceives and recognizes the prescription of divine law, making one capable of recognizing the moral quality of the act that conscience is going to perform, is performing, or has already been completed. So, humans are obliged to follow such virtuous norms, which in turn puts them on an ideal path. The truth about morality stated in the law of reasons suggests that all individuals should refrain from causing harm to each other's liberty, prosperity and well-being.

Humans have a conscience with a sense of what is right and what is evil, but it is observed that everyone's conscience does not function alike, which is due to the environment in which one lives and interacts with others for their livelihood and the literature they read. It is asserted that conscience plays a role of telling us what we ought to do and guiding us in our lives. It serves as a source of moral knowledge and acts as motivation, getting us ready for situations that are not only difficult but may even pose life threats.

Being conscience is a very noble and subtle act of having a rational and helping attitude at an appropriate time while keeping into consideration the preferences of each individual. The function of our existence is to put us in contact with our universal nature, with the objective truth, with God, or with whatever one thinks comfortable with it. It is observed that one acts according to one's mind, heart and conscience; all are spiritual entities and well interconnected with the soul of every human being. Whereas the role of conscience, as per scripture, is to harmonize thinking and feeling so that actions are for the welfare of society because truth and goodness are the definition of God. God expects us to be responsible and caretakers of our souls and He also expects that we must live in accordance with His will, as this is the only way to have peace of mind and a perfect life. But people do not respond this way, which is due to the human races. Race in this materialistic world, which is a main cause of troubles in our livelihood. Everyone is unhappy. People who have no faith in God, are not aligned with His agenda, take goodness and righteousness just as the word of the dictionary and act self-centered get the mind absorbed in the lie of unbelief when the conscience has no resource to resist all these. This is due to the environment in which we spend more time and make relationships with those who keep violations a routine matter for living. This leads us to a corrupt life, resulting in a decrease in health and ultimately to death, which nobody wants. It is also a fact that this does not last long and puts one under stress to think that what has happened, which has gone wrong and should be avoided in the future. This way, we get to recognize our sins, which have polluted our conscience, taken us so far from God and put us in anxiety. To get rid of such sins that have destroyed the soul, as every activity is with the consent of the soul and to clean the conscience, the only way is to follow God's norms. This makes us understand the proper working of the conscience and nurture and maintain our conscience in the best working order. We should never do evil so that there exists a good; therefore, it is right not to do anything that makes us stumble.

The philosopher asserted and considered conscience a pivot of moral life whose fragrance one observes in many sorts, such as obeying divine laws, acting as per prevalent situations, etc. Adopting this tradition, one considered that conscience is a commandment in life, but as per scripture, it is a pre-critical methodology and asserted that whatever one's is today, divine get emerge in it accordingly, within humanity's sense as the core of that sense, not as its commandments but a duty, the duty one does with senses, it means willingness, that is, there is some specific purpose such as to run a life. Therefore, senses are supposed to be basic to our conscience prior to even our principles and when one does, one has a feeling of conscience. It is believed that whenever any emotional happening takes place, conscience comes into existence to take the appropriate action. Often, it is observed that whenever one needs help while no one turns out for help or another person is not helping out when they should, their conscience gets it instantaneously. Empathy, gratitude, fairness, compassion and pride are all examples of emotions that encourage us to do something for others. The emotions that stop actions for others are guilt, shame, embarrassment and a fear of being judged poorly by others. It gets understood that conscience acts as an opener to our awareness, which clarifies that ignorance of conscience is ignorance of the moral universe in which humans are qualitatively different from objects and by virtue of this quality, humans have claims on us and on each other. Behaving normally and calmly requires adopting the characteristics of conscience. The philosopher asserted that the basic part of being a human being is helping others and keeping track of those who help us to make us a well-rounded human being. Conscience is a natural phenomenon of keeping the individual aware of any unlawful activities and getting them summarized for the conscience, soul, mind and intellect, as all are invisible, but one cannot have one's life without them and all have an important aspect in the life of a human being. So, to grasp the study of the conscience, the study of all these may be imperative for a human being.

Conscience and the universe: we regret doing wrong work and feel satisfied doing a good job. Everyone experiences this and we call it the reality of conscience. The universe is everything; it comprises actions that are due to certain reasons, it took the person to the destination and we call it a journey of life. The journey of life is very much connected with the conscience and is interdependent. But the scholars and scientists consider this a process of the brain; this theory is not more than two hundred years old, whereas our old scripture, which is the oldest among all scriptures, has given this the name of conscience. The soul that exists in humans is prescribed by God's law. In every human, there exists a sense of holiness, righteousness and good things, depending upon the extent to which our mind, heart and conscience are serving God's intend. This shows that humans are an image of God and does such acts that, being rational to all, there is a need to understand a rational process and the way the rational process takes part in human vitality. A rational process is a logic expressing a fundamental mode of being human; it is a rational process which keeps us to a sense of being human and shows us how differently and appropriately one's actions are. There are three such rational processes, or fundamental ways of our being.

i. Theoretical reasons, pursuing truth
ii. Practical reasons, pursuing the good
iii. Relational reasons, pursuing human connections.

These processes are rational, so they involve reasons, considerations in favor of some goals, that is, the truth, the good, or connection. A soul that gives life to humans is created by God; it is an energy, a life force, having the property of being undestroyable, invisibility and never dying. It only changes from one state to another, but it is never created nor destroyed. It is eternal and an independent, subtle elements are directly under the control of God.

Consciousness. This refers to awareness and awakening in human's internal and external activities and is most probably considered as a function of the mind, the mind in which thoughts, feelings, ideas, memories and opinions are being processed by the act of perception, experience, imagination, reasoning, or believing, refining it and then storing it or rejecting it. The awareness is defined by the content of consciousness and awakening by the level of consciousness. Sri Aurobindo, an Indian philosopher, yogi, maharishi, poet and Indian nationalist, narrated consciousness as: It is not only the power of awareness of self and things but also a dynamic and creative energy. In addition, it is not simply a yes or no phenomenon but puts us into a manifesting hierarchy ranging from the seeming obliviousness of matter below to the seemingly super conscient Spirit above. That is, all three aspects of consciousness - its cosmic nature, its energy aspect and its ability to differentiate itself into varying forms and degrees - combine to produce the process of involution and evolution of consciousness; it is the character of consciousness. It is observed that the more information one is able to gather and process, the more aware and the more conscious one becomes. The conscious one is in a perpetual state of learning; it leads one to learn how to describe and re-describe its own activity to itself. The Indian philosophers (Rishis) were the first to probe into the nature of consciousness. They used meditative processes to study consciousness subjectivity and objectivity to explore the hidden powers and potency of the mind to make it available for human welfare and self-transformation. Consciousness is fundamentally subjective, as it is the inner experience of an individual having no facts. It becomes objective only when it is commonly held perceptions and awareness. The Indian philosophers asserted that their purpose in doing so was to study the status of reality according to the mind. No doubt, reality is a product of the mind or exists on its own without the mind and the senses. They studied the limitations of the mind to see the world with better clarity and awareness. It is the Yogic view of the mind, in which one observes the mind rather than follows its reactions. It takes us to understand the process of perception and its actions toward us. The Yoga tradition took the mind to the highest prospective, which is called "chitta" in Sanskrit, encompassing all aspects of conditioned consciousness. It includes reason, emotion, sensation, memory, the instinctual part of the mind and the ego. It is asserted that we all have a certain level of consciousness, but under the concept of chitta, one becomes capable of higher creativity and intuition beyond the personal mind and physical consciousness, which only a few people may develop significantly. Chitta promotes the person beyond the personal mind to collective and cosmic aspects of the mind, giving the person a mind akin to a cosmic principle. Yoga regards consciousness as "chit," something other than the mind or chitta. The philosophers asserted that the mind is an instrument of thinking and sensing on various levels and is called the inner instrument, related to the body, which is our outer instrument. Chit is pure consciousness, unaltered by any mental activities. According to our ancient scriptures, there is consciousness in everything and consciousness arises through the interactions of matter and soul, enabling every organism to make decisions and it is directly related to the soul. Therefore, the soul is consciousness, which means it has senses of thoughts, feelings, emotions and relations and we call this the physical body. The soul is considered a spiritual subtle element with the faculties of intelligence and will and we call it a subtle body. The soul, in blissful consciousness, in the awareness principle, is called the causal body. The soul receives energy from space and interacts with the brain to reach its destination, demonstrating that the soul is well aware of all actions. The soul, in association with nature, acts as the preserver or upholder of creation through the process of degenerative involution and regenerative evolution. The individual soul, in association with nature, acts as an embodied soul or "jivas." Nature weaves its web of deception and illusion around the soul, causing it to become entangled in this materialistic world and forget its own role. The soul lacks a memory system to store knowledge; it instantaneously experiences the reality under consideration with complete awareness of the moment. The individual soul, considered subjective because it is entirely self-absorbed, becomes objective when it comes in contact with the things of nature. In this state, the soul experiences the duality of subject and object, leading to the loss of its transcendental self-awareness property. It becomes entangled with various impurities and develops corresponding qualities and abilities, such as intelligence, mind, desires and aversions. It also indulges in egoistic and selfish actions, which leads to the philosophy of Karma, binding it in the cycle of births and deaths and enslaving it to the force of nature. According to our ancient scriptures, the soul is unique and different from others and its size may vary.

Chit is awareness, often called the Purusha, the inner being, for which the mind is a tool of perception and expression. Yoga similarly regards the mind and brain, though they are different but well interconnected. The brain acts as the hardware of a computer, whereas the mind is the CPU of the computer. Purusha is our inner self, while the mind and body could be seen as internal and external instruments, but they are not our real identity. The light that enables the mind to function comes from the Purusha; the mind has no light of its own. Our sense of self, the understanding that we are unique, whole and an active center of awareness, arises from inner consciousness, not from the mind. The Yogic perspective on the mind is slightly different. It is asserted that a person's mental state is influenced by their physical well-being and the condition of the mind is linked to the condition of the body. Therefore, a person's quality of life depends on the condition of the mind. The mind inherently possesses psychological characteristics because it is a product of time and outer experiences, which leave their imprints on the mind. In Ayurveda and Yogic psychology, these imprints are well classified based on qualities (sattva, rajas, Tamas), doshas (vata, pitta and kapha) and other energetic factors. In contrast, our true self or Purusha lacks psychological factors because it is unconditioned consciousness, existing outside of time and beyond the influence of the mind. It transcends all forms and qualities, while the mind engages in mental activities. The inner being consists of pure, unmodified awareness only. It means that if we delve deeply into our awareness of our inner being, it enlightens our consciousness and leads us beyond all psychological suffering. Therefore, the ultimate Yogic solution to psychological problems is to elevate our awareness to the inner consciousness beyond the mind and its dualities. Other factors, such as diet, behavior, breath and the senses, have proven to be useful in enhancing our awareness, ultimately leading to a revolution in our consciousness. This shift takes us from a mind-based consciousness to pure consciousness, from chitta to chit.

In my view, consciousness represents an ideal state that elevates individuals to heights they aspire to but only a few people achieve. This is the path to attaining salvation, which is the highest goal in a human's life. Being conscious reflects a person's good character and is admired by the masses. The voice of the masses is often considered the voice of God, so following consciousness means adhering to God's principles, which is essential. All these aspects are subtle in nature but hold utmost importance in human life.

The Vedas are the root of all knowledge and are at the forefront as our guide. One who goes through these scriptures is considered a virtuous and noble person, as it is understood that the person having the knowledge of the Vedas acts as a guide to others in the complete discipline of life. Next comes the duty to die. The third is the conduct of the great sages of the past. Fourth are the examples of the virtuous people of our own time and last is conscience, which defines the duty of the human. Now, people decide their duty as per their conscience, not as per the Vedas, which have a written verdict, but it is being observed that one gets consulted by conscience only when one has no other means of knowing one's duty as per one's action, so, in this way, when one has no other way of taking decisions, conscience is being called one's "manahsaksi" which means a witness. As a witness, it gives us true reports, but on this basis, one cannot reach a degree of finality as everybody is right as per their conscience, which is not a justification of one's duty or a right attitude. The philosophers asserted that the conscience, in its individual and universal aspects, is viewed as a conscience, which one understands as an innate, intuitive faculty that determines the perception of right and wrong, given the name of intuitionism. Conscience, which one understands as cumulative, subjective and applying one's experience to decide the future, is what one calls empiricism. As per our oldest scripture, the Vedas, the mind, whose driver is the man himself, is constituted by three sheaths. i) the physical body; ii) the energy or soul; iii) the thoughts or intellect. The physical body is the requirement for any action to be taken, the energy to run the physical body and the intellect to keep the state of equilibrium and balance. All three sheaths are interrelated, where the energy or soul acts as a medium of exchange for the psycho-physiological system. These three sheaths often act as one to whom we refer. The mind is constituted by five basic components:

i. Manas, or thoughts; sensory impressions, which one obtains from sensory organs, that is, by seeing, touching, hearing, smelling and tasting an object; and confirming the object under consideration before utilizing the sensory information. The information is utilized by the consciousness of the one.

ii. Ahamkara, or ego, is the senses of an individual that relate to the identity of one's functioning and one thinks it is a distinct and separate quality. This acts as a source of intelligence, which favors the development of nature.

This awareness of intelligence gives birth to ahamkara, or ego consciousness and its evaluation is derived from the intellect.

iii. Citta, or conscious, means "to perceive." Consciousness is the space that holds all perceivable things. Swami Vivekananda defined citta as a tool through which the external world is perceived. We call this a store of the mind's knowledge.

iv. Buddhi, or intellect, is a kind of knowledge that exists in all of us and helps us in running our lives; it puts us at an authority where one discriminates and decides what is good for us and what is not. It is the intellect where one makes use of one's experience appropriately to regulate one's life and behavior. Wisdom is an essential aspect for humans, whereas humans without intellect used to be considered foolish.

v. Atman, or soul, discussed in the first paragraph.

CHAPTER - 3

Evolution

There are many theories of conscience, some of which suggest that conscience is theologically implanted. This is true as everything is by the grace of God; God created the universe and all the creatures, distinguishing humans from other species as humans have the senses of right and wrong. Conscience, which we consider the voice of God, always acted rightly, but sometimes it acted so heinously that we felt ashamed. This is due to the fact that God acts differently for different people, identifying a difference between good and bad, which may be an obvious one as everyone has their own actions as per their own will, resulting in a difference in their own Karma, whereas we get rewards, that is, happiness or sorrow, as per our Karma. So, it is obvious that God has acted differently toward everyone. Some say that God being eternal, their voice may be eternal, unchanging and must be the same for all persons at all times. The variation needs to be examined to see if it happened. Some say God always helps all without discrimination. God lives within us as impulsiveness, conscious of us in all our actions and fulfilling our needs as and when required. So, opposing the decision of God is to give importance to non-relevant thoughts. So, the characteristics of the conscience are in accordance with the divine laws and we must act accordingly.

Some suggest that conscience is very much related to one's hereditary heritage and consider this the "voice of the hereditary". Hereditary evolution is a biological process that has the characteristic of passing one's ancestral wisdom, whether it is good or bad, to the baby, which is the by-product of the two souls. This way, each species survives and develops inheritable tendencies, enabling the baby to adopt through innate response patterns. These are called "instincts". Each creature, whether human or animal, is born with innate tendencies, although one also adopts the habits of one's own environment. Conscience basically consists of inheritance, but it gets matured when humans mature, that is, when they have knowledge of the external world and internal life. Some suggest that conscience is axiologically inherent. Presently, we are in an era where there is chaos and chaos; nobody is comfortable, though there is a good flow of education through which the economy automatically grows; even then, we are all uncomfortable. In my view, we are lacking patience and ethics. It is the patience that finds out the way to our problems, thus keeping us tension-free and it is the ethics that teaches us the way of life, thus keeping us socially strong so that we may have a friendly environment. There is a need to seek the value of the entity, not the price, the values that refer to the original faculty of intellect, emotions and will which are centered at the heart, which means centered at the absolute God. The heart is the seat of the soul and the soul is an element of God.

The philosophy of axiology, which is existential, theistic and dialogic in nature, has made an attempt to present a view of values that makes conscience a part of it. The theory asserts that intellect, emotions and will refer to the values of trueness, goodness and beauty, respectively. Trueness refers to the concept of education, which has a crucial role in the development of knowledge; goodness refers to the concept of ethics; and will refers to the concept of beauty, which is the basic requirement for realization. The realization that took humans to their destination acts as "the right," which tends to promote the development at all their capacities. The theory asserted that values remain an asset of the living that illuminate one's life and there are no absolute, objective, or subjective values. The values of one's life get increased by interaction with different societies. So, the conscience, which has the capacity to define ethics, whose knowledge-based acts are always considered to be right and authentic and the source of this knowledge, which is not yet known. The source of knowledge being speculated by different theories leads to the conclusion that axiological theory, which is a value-based theory, has also attempted and created a base for dialogue to reach the destination.

Some suggest that conscience is a function of the brain. The brain, which has many segments, is responsible for its respective function and is well connected with the soul, mind and spirit, though each one does not occupy any space. The interaction between the brain and the soul is due to the actions of the physical body and nature, which give birth to consciousness and remain active till we survive in this world. This consciousness makes one aware of himself internally as well as externally; this awareness, which is beyond consciousness, leads one's conscience to judge the differences between right and wrong, the judgment that is the conclusion of the reasoning process. The conscience, by its intellect, which is the faculty of the soul, utilizes the perception of mind through the senses; these senses in the brain give birth to "intellect," which the brain submits to the soul through the senses. So, some consider the conscience a function of the brain. However, the concept of conscience is being taken as a deeply held moral knowledge of the self. Conscience means making accurate judgments; judgments are made by determinants, determinants by intellect and intellect is the reality of knowledge. So, the conscience is the extract of all these forming an act, which we call the voice of the soul or the conscience. Knowledge is in the self in an immaterial way, comes from a number of levels or from combination and transcends this knowledge to the soul or mind through the senses for judgment and reasons.

The conscience, which acts as a soul, forming judgments that are spiritual operations, always thinks rationally as long as we remain alive. The rise of conscience in the higher sense is due to one's intuitive knowledge; it gets raised as per one's age, supported by spiritual inspiration. Consciousness, that is, speculated to be, is God's gift occupying no space; the physical body gets integrated with this space and remains active as long as one's living. It is speculated that the existence of the spaceless conscience in the physical body is where the physical heart is placed. Conscience is a function of consciousness, whereas consciousness is a property of the brain. Conscience is an enlightened intellect, a form of formless mind, that helps to decide our actions. The actions are "Karma," which are proportional to our consciousness. It is very much astonishing to note that one gets motivated by the inner senses, that is, the conscience of moral rightness and wrongness, but not by the external acting of rightness and wrongness. The philosopher asserted that it is never right to go against conscience; they studied the people who go against moral principles based on external authority; on the other hand, such people are very loyal to their duties because of their own perception of right and wrong. The philosopher categorized the people as per their actions, such as the people whose status and rights are guaranteed by human laws in the ethical world; next, the people who are acting ethically individually; this is also a good culture; next, the people who are self-conscious; their actions are for specific purposes in a particular situation; they differ from ethical individuality and in combining individuality and universality. The one who acts from conscience knows and does what is absolutely right, keeping himself displaced from the moral worldview, making the difference between duty and reality and favoring the individual consciousness that knows that it has its truth in the immediate certainty (conscience) of itself.

There is a difference between the moral worldview and the self of conscience. In the moral worldview, the subject is the moral laws that one obeys, whereas the self of conscience is the act whose contents reflect the objective elements that are universal and recognized. This is due to the knowledge of the self, which is an important aspect of the self's conscience. All actions require knowledge; the knowledge we count as moral essentiality or duty, being useful to others in need, is a pure duty. Pure duty, or pure knowing, is the character of conscience that leads one to good actions for others. The action of conscience is not only the specific action but also the action of one's own knowledge; this keeps one as a duty of one's knowledge and shows the distinction between the act and the acting. Conscience has the capability of knowing and doing which act is necessary to apply at that specific time; it knows the inner voice, which is known to be a divine voice. As such, one can assess one's duty and may equate it with the divine's duty, which rectifies one's to being a human being, which is the goal of a human being. It is conscience when one has the authority to grant the irrevocable loss to the deserving one but denies it due to non-proper documentation. In such a situation, the authority's compassion prompts its conscience to make some arrangements for the deserving one. Conscience gives one a moral force that is, far superior to the brute force. The philosopher asserted the concept of "superego," which has a role in explaining conscience as it regulates one's conduct and plays an important role in moral +development. The human is morally bound by conscience. Conscience is considered a mental activity that regulates impartiality and self, whereas the superego is also a concept of the mind and regulates the system of one's life. So, it is believed that the superego reflects the identity of a human, such as conduct, behavior, etc. It becomes necessary to go through the topic so that one can assess the values of the superego. The superego is the ego of another superimposed on one's own, the ego, which is considered the identity of the human being and is regulated by, firstly, the demands of society and secondly, the materialistic world has accepted this.

According to Freud, a philosopher, the superego is the social component of one's personality, represented by one's conscience and is based on the ideal of perfection. One's personality consists of identity, ego and superego, all of which are put together to make a complete personality. The superego is the social component and is one's conscience. In psychology, the superego is further divided into two components: the ego ideal and the conscience. The ego ideal includes the rules and standards for good behavior that are authorized by competent authority; they may be as inscribed in our old scripture or as enforced by the government from time-to-time as per the prevailing situations. whereas conscience is composed of rules that put one to happiness when one's actions tally with the ideal ego and one feels ashamed when one's actions are bad, which conscience considers bad. The superego exists in all three stages: consciousness (our present awareness), pre-consciousness (knowledge and memories we can retrieve) and unconsciousness (outside of awareness at all times). The primary action of the superego is to act for moral perfection and discard the actions of those that are unacceptable to society; that is, it acts as a regulation system of the self-based on relational turn and neuropsychoanalysis, whereas the conscience also regulates the self, paying paramount importance to the nature of the self. The primary function of the conscience is to ensure the stability of the self. The self is in reality a system of self-states that determines how self may develops. In the superego, the first self-experience one observes is in the form of attachments and emotions between child and caretaker, leading to an implicit self to whom we refer.

This also gives birth to empathy, which boosts the developmental perspective of the self. Empathy is not an emotion or feeling itself, but a mental activity that helps in evaluating the self. It is capable of experiencing the emotions of others in addition to its own emotions. It is a natural activity to have the ability to understand and share the feelings of others. Conceptualizing the self in relation to the conscience means imparting emotions and feelings to the developing child, which ultimately crystallizes into the adult identity, thus summarizing the self and keeping himself fit in understanding the function of the conscience, that is, self-conscious emotions. The function of the conscience and the function of the superego are almost similar and are most probably co-dependent, as the conscience first regulates self-conscious emotions and the lateral regulates self-basic emotions. Conscious emotions indicate the right and wrong aspects of the action, whereas basic emotions, though they are also right, indicate the status of the emotions. There are many different ideas about the conscience, but the conscience is so diverse and complex that one can have a long discussion on this. So, to overcome all these, one must follow the text of our old scripture, which is considered divine.

CHAPTER - 4

Philosophy

The concept of conscience has the following aspects:

1. Conscience is pluralistic, neutral and subjective; it might have been noticed that conscience makes different suggestions to different people, that is, as per the prevailing situation. This shows that there is no psychological or conceptual relationship between conscience and any particular moral belief. This independence of the notion of conscience from any substantial moral content can be understood by following the three senses.

   i. Firstly, the pluralistic notion means that conscience is subject to multiple acts in order to save the sanctity of conscience. The function of the conscience is to act rightly, for which the conscience has to sense the activity and then act accordingly. This means the act of the conscience may violate one, but it might be the right of another. For example, "honesty is above all." It is a fact, a virtue, but as per Acharya Chanakya, the straight trees are cut first, that is, the honest person is the first sufferer, which is a violation. So, conscience acts as a pluralistic way to avoid violations.

   ii. Secondly, a neutral concept the characteristic of conscience is to act as per the divine's law; there is neither favoritism nor any suffering of one's rights; it acts as a neutral. So, the decision of conscience is considered as full and final as the decisions are to the mark.

iii. Thirdly, the subjective concept of conscience is considered subjective as it is the belief of an individual that may be right or wrong. The belief is one's mind exercise, which generally favors the individual; moreover, it depends upon the status of the mind at the time of the mind's exercise, so it does not suit all. These three aspects show the independence of conscience.

2. Conscience as self-knowledge and self-assessment When we discuss conscience, it means we are discussing the morality of a human, the human who possesses the knowledge of right and wrong, the knowledge which one has acquired from hereditary, its own and which one has gained by one's experience over the years, plays a crucial role in taking decisions on account of right and wrong conduct. This knowledge of right and wrong, we call it a conscience, is by which we examine ourselves, as it is observed that the individual gets himself differentiated into two groups: one is the actor and the other is the examiner who examines the actor's conduct. It is believed that the problem in question is being shared with God for solution; it acts as an inner judge and makes its judgments accordingly, whereas the conscience to which we imagined and a fact acts as an impartial spectator. The character of the conscience is to present a moral judgment about one's and its actions and act as a witness to the Divine's laws. The laws that the authorities have suggested and these acts as universal laws get enforced on the public for the welfare of all. Everyone thinks that one's actions are right because they are as per one's own conscience; one's is adjusting its feelings and judgment as

per one's conscience standard, whereas when we think of the consciences of others, we usually act as a subjective moral standard. This asymmetry shows that there is no conceptual relation between the notion of conscience and the notion of an objective or the correct moral standard. It is understood that conscience has merely to act with one's private morality and one's commitment to one's own morality. It is observed that conscience, which acts as a judge in deciding morality issues, possesses a sense of feeling. When conscience acts as a self-evaluating subtle matter, it is considered that conscience may be conceived of either as constituted by such self-evaluating feelings or as occasioning them. Conscience as constituted by self-evaluative feeling means feeling with cognitive content, where the cognitive content means the adherence of one's behavior to a certain moral standard. Conscience as occasioning self-evaluative feelings: when one's conscience is under stress due to the wrong conduct of others, it generates negative feelings. A human being, a moral constraint, takes "the form of conscience" to exercise its control over self and instincts by producing negative evaluative feelings toward others who have shown misconduct. These self-directed negative feelings generate motivational force within the individual, which plays an essential role in fulfilling the motivational function of the conscience. Self-assessment and motivation make one's strong morality, which is not only consistent with one another but actually completes one another. It is considered that conscience is most often associated with negative feelings; this is not the case; the fact is, the truth is always bitter. So, to make it joyful, the joy did not come from self-praise or pride but from the following of God's law; the best among them is "Do good and Have good." Joy comes into one's life.

3. Conscience as a faculty of direct and indirect moral knowledge. Conscience, which we have understood as the internal knowledge base faculty of humans, is what informs us about moral knowledge or moral beliefs, either in an absolute sense that means the knowledge of the divine laws or in a relative sense that is, the knowledge of the social norms in one's culture. Conscience, which gives us moral knowledge, does not provide us direct access to the source of this knowledge, as it is understood that this knowledge is often conceived as mediated knowledge. The understanding of the conscience as having an epistemic function and its role were discussed here: As a faculty for direct moral knowledge, conscience itself is such a complex and deeper study of moral knowledge that the study is unable to access the source of knowledge. So, the philosopher asserted that it is considered that the knowledge that conscience has access to us is already within us and we acquire it through other processes not involving conscience, such as divine intervention. Education is also one of the sources that keeps one's conscience away from the corrupting influences of society and it is by virtue of nature that conscience follows the right order of nature. A good teacher acts as a catalyst in a young person's conscience to follow the path of nature, which persuades one to obey one's conscience. The understanding of conscience as a deeper form of moral knowledge brings one to the second sense in which conscience can be said to have an epistemic role, that is, witnessing, receiving opinions, or divine laws. Conscience can also be conceived as a moral sense, giving one's direct access to moral principles. It is understood that conscience is a faculty of moral knowledge possessing intuitive senses and feelings of emotion with no accessibility to logic and reasons. So, the conformity of this active conscience becomes faint with

the inactivity of reasons. Reasoning is part of morality and neuroscience makes it possible and suggests that our most fundamental moral beliefs might be based on intuitions and emotions over which our rational capacities have little control. If this context proves to be correct, then we have reasons that these intuitions and emotions may have effects on our conscience. People do have the belief that any moral belief might be supported by reasons, so that its justification may be sought. Theoretically, we have a right to doubt her, but conscience never deceives us; it is the true guide of a human. One who follows one's conscience means following nature, which means not being afraid that one will go astray. So, the reasons and evidence have no importance for conscience. It is observed that when we heed the voice of conscience, we find joy in the answer of a good conscience; we too can call it direct access to moral knowledge.

Conscience as a faculty for indirect moral knowledge gives us the idea that conscience can be conceived as fulfilling an introspective function, that is, as being directed toward the self and toward one's own mental states. Introspection acts as a process of acquiring self-knowledge, but the self, which is considered to be equipped with moral laws, the laws that are part of one's body, becomes the objective of introspection. The word introspection can replace the word conscience if the acts are rational. So, a treasury of good and true has been established within one to whom we call a conscience, which acts as an inner sense having a capacity to recall one's actions; if one ignores conscience on himself, he hears its echo from within. The philosopher asserted that this is the voice of God echoing in the form of conscience in each of us. This shows that conscience acts as only a witness and does not have any direct epistemic access to the source of knowledge, that is, to God. Conscience is the act of applying universal principles (divine laws) to real-life situations; divine law is the inborn knowledge of the primary principle of morality of the individual. On this account, conscience might fail in deriving moral conclusions from primary principles. On a secular account, the external source of moral knowledge that keeps moral principles within one is not God but one's own culture or upbringing. Conscience is the faculty through which social norms or the norms of one's upbringing are evoked and put into influence on one's moral psychology. Conscience gives us the product of social and cultural dynamics over which we have little control. It means we are bound by our social and cultural systems, which shows that conscience is a relativistic notion whose content varies as per our society, so it acts as a faculty for indirect moral knowledge.

4. Conscience as motivation to act morally. Motivation is the key to success in reaching any destination. Conscience, which is an invisible part of the body and by which everyone seeks a sense of duty to adopt the character of conscience to make himself an ideal for others, must be the aim of life. Conscience, which is subjective in character, makes the individual stand for their own words, which is only possible when one sticks to the character of conscience. The character of conscience is moral-based where every act is understood as full of morality. Morality is an asset to human beings and conscience acts as a motivational force for human beings to adopt the culture of morality. Conscience is a source of pleasure or displeasure in relation to the quality of the morality with which one complies. When one complied with morality, this motivates one's to act in this sense rather than others, which leads to displeasure. It is observed that one feels ashamed when one commits a violation, whereas nobody wants to be

ashamed. In this way, conscience acts as a motivational force that compels one to act as a moral human being. Sometimes negative feelings get generated in ourselves by our previous actions, which means we move to a former state and negative emotions get around us. To overcome such a state, we must move to our fundamental moral education that has constituted our conscience. It is by nature that humans are bound by morals and their actions are all morally bound. The conscience, which plays a role in awakening to act rightly in human activities, possesses an important position, that is, in building a human being. The human is rational and its actions are always positive, as one's actions are as per one's sense of duty, which is the basic quality of the human.

5. Conscience, a self-identifying moral commitment and moral integrity, Conscience is a part of the human body possessing no space, but the role of conscience is so vital that it assesses every activity of a human, whether it is social or political. Socially means how much one sticks to one's conscience, that is, considering conscience supreme. Whereas politically, we are here concerned with the principle of respect for moral integrity, the justification of which one observes in the close relationship between the notions of conscience and moral integrity. Notion of conscience means the conscience by heart; it means the personal identity that is the quality of a particular person, whereas moral integrity refers to our faithfulness toward morality, that is, our commitment to the morality for which our life is meant, which we call conscience. Conscience as self-identifying refers to either a set of self-identifying moral beliefs or a way of approaching and relating to such moral beliefs, that is, a commitment to uphold one's such concept and a mode of consciousness in which prospective actions are viewed in relation to one's self and his character.

In either way, conscience is a measure that determines the quality of a person. This gives us a sense of how much conscience is important for us and how much we have to take care of conscience as well as its sanctity.

6. Conscience is a trustworthy guide only when it is informed and ruled by God. To violate one's conscience is indeed a sin, but what makes something a sin is choosing our own will over the will of God. So, our conscience is only trustworthy when it does not lead us to choose our will over the will of God. Sometimes conscience is misinformed; the reason for this is that the informed person is reluctant to study the verdict of God. This misinformation leads to violation, or we advocate for violation, which is a sin, an injection into the sanctity of the conscience. Our conscience is a witness to reality and truth and we are guilty of sin when we ignore this reality and act according to our sense of reality. To willfully act against the conscience is always a sin. The human, who is understood as God's element, is supposed to follow the divine rules, whereas it is observed to be the reverse of this. It is due to the outlook of the human being that one prefers to fit in the environment that suits him. Secondly, humans, being social animals, try to interact with maximum numbers to gain social and political status. This maximum number is of different ideologies; it may be good or bad and humans also have the quality of adopting the culture in which they are associated. In this way, one becomes addicted to such habits that are against conscience, though one takes it easy as one has accepted them willfully and does not feel any guilt in doing such acts, but action against conscience is a sin that should be avoided. One should keep a distance from immature people, as they don't have faith in our eternal scripture. A philosopher wrote very correctly on this: "It is neither right nor safe to act against the conscience".

7. Conscience can be suppressed by sin. The good and bad are two aspects of the same coin; it's up to him to decide which one should be followed. The good have no physical shine, but their sanctity illuminates the darkness of the evil, whereas the bad have a physical shine that is momentary and can be lost at any time; that is, it has no footing. If one wants to develop a good culture in himself, one has to remain involved in actions that yield positive outcomes, benefiting the maximum. One must accept this as a part of life until it becomes an automatic reflex. In this way, similar things happen when one falls into a sin. Accepting sin means rejecting God's authority. If one repeats the sin, over time, the rejection of God's authority becomes an automatic reflex. When one rejects God's authority, it means one is doubting the existence of God, which is the very reality of God, such as its invisible attribute; our all-vital natural resources running well in time show the existence of God. The action is related to unrighteousness, which means suppressing the truth; the individual always believes that his or her actions are correct, which is a mistake in individualism. Sin makes one's conscience seared, corrupted and wholly unreliable, so one must protect one's conscience by not indulging himself in unrighteous and irrational actions.

Freedom of conscience: Conscience, which has a capacity to assess every activity of the one, that is, the personal identity of the one. Personal identity means the quality of a person and it is the quality of a person that how comfortably one's come out of the living crises of the life as the living life in context to socially, politically and economically, which one's have to go through all these to live a comfortable life, as one wants to pace with the society, it bears a complex task, so, as it is being called, life is a bundle of crises. One uses this personal identity to carry out political missions. The political uses of conscience have given this the name of the principle of freedom of conscience. There are three main reasons to apply the concept of the principle of freedom of conscience.

i. We generally observed a lot of difference between the act and the action, which is due to the fact that everyone is free to exercise their knowledge. We can't compel someone to believe or not to believe something; changing someone's beliefs by compelling is what we term hypocritical behavior, which is undesirable and objectionable. This reflects that one is prohibiting one's free expression of one's conscience. Philosophically, freedom of conscience is an individual's concept that allows one to choose their beliefs as per their conscience and not as per the external forces that influence or compel them to accept the norms as per their thoughts. It has been observed that forcing someone to accept a particular belief has no effects on one's conscience. The philosopher asserted that one should not ignore this reason, that is, ineffectiveness, in order to justify imposing norms and practices that might violate an individual's conscience. It must be noted that the same reasons, that is, ineffectiveness, can be used to support the imposition of policies that might conflict with an individual's conscience. On the basis of the idea that conscience is merely a matter of private beliefs, not of action, the philosopher asserted that forcing people to follow their norms, whether it is against their conscience, does not constitute a violation of their freedom of conscience and is therefore justifiable. This may suit someone or not, but it protects the social order.

ii. Reasons for ignorance: are based on the concept that the content of conscience may require discussion and not simply acceptance. Some believe that the contents of conscience, which one believes, may be wrong and the holding of conscientious beliefs opposite to ours are right. Therefore, there exists a reason for not forcing anyone to accept a particular belief that may be considered morally wrong. In my view, we term this ignorance of conscience; we are born by conscience, so compelling someone to accept a particular belief is not freedom of conscience.

iii. Reasons for legitimization: this is to defend freedom of conscience with the concept that allowing the free expression of any opinion, particularly mistaken opinions, leads to emerging the truth more clearly and provides us with a justification for acting upon our own beliefs, which were once assessed against other opinions. Contradicting and disapproving one's opinion is a logic that justifies one's assumption of truth for the purpose of actions. Moreover, this is the only human faculty that has a rational assurance of being right.

Part 3

Values

CHAPTER - 1

Significance

V**alues**. India is a country where values are considered to be the most important, as in our ancient literature, where we see the reflection of our rich culture (values and virtues) in our ancient India. Our ancient scholars, whom we call Rishis, taught their disciples morals and human values through their teachings, preaching and writings. Shrimad Bhagwat Gita, our old spiritual text, is the best example of this topic, text, having the biggest number of followers in the world. Acharya Vidur Niti and Acharya Chanakya Niti comprise literature on morals and human values, which are most prevalent in modern times. In spite of such rich literature, it is being observed that a great deterioration of human values in human society has taken place. A great example of this is the climate change caused by global warming, which is due to the human fault. It is asserted that human society cannot sustain itself without human values, so it becomes the duty of humans to raise awareness of human values in society to save mankind.

The Vedas and Upanishads describe the duty of humans. The first and foremost duty of humans is to save nature. They put stress on education. Education makes us capable of understanding the concept of human values, their characteristics and studying them accordingly, making us ideal humans. Therefore, it is asserted that there exists a relationship between human values and value education. According to Swami Vivekananda "Education is the manifestation of perfection; it exists already in man". Swamiji asserted that the purpose of education is not only taken in terms of knowledge, understanding and skill but also in terms of human values and motives, which are the significance of one's behavior and conduct in society, a kind of quality in humans that humans make use of while performing activities.

Significance of human values: It plays a vital role in a human's life, as these are the basis for humans, which leads the individual to a better life. Value education starts right from childhood with parents, then in school with educators and later in the environment where we are associated with our profession to earn a peaceful living. It imparts to us, that value is a theory that makes us capable of recognizing which things in the world are good, desirable and important, which leads to a quality life. Values are a mixture of three concepts; these are explained as:

i. **Ideas**. Idea or concept: Ideas are thoughts, but not all thoughts are ideas. When an innovation is sought out in the mind of a human, it is associated with the thought or intellect or the question of the concept. It gets enroute through the soul, which is the subtle body of God and has consciousness in everything, but it must be understood that every idea that comes out should have a righteous act. But all ideas are not good; the ideas that have the support of the masses are termed good ideas, whereas the ideas that have ill effects are termed bad ideas, that is, not supported by the masses. One should not be afraid of such acts; one should discard them and get in touch with others; ultimately, one will get a good idea. It is also true that every idea possesses a good thought or idea.

ii. **Quality**. Quality, refers to virtue, which everyone has, more or less, however it may be everyone wish, that, one **to** be known by a good qualitative one as it recognizes the good identity of humans. So, it has become the perception of the human mind that it likes qualitative people because they have rational thinking, which everyone wants. As a result, they asked everyone to accept the specific good and acknowledge it. So, it has many definitions; it may be subjective as well as objective depending upon the needs and the environment, such as: it is the assurance of an entity's characteristics and its ability; it is the basic tool in assessing the natural property of an entity or service by being compared with other entities or services of the same kind; it is the value of an entity that meets the expectations of the person; it is the degree to which an entity fulfills the specified set of attributes or requirements and so many more. In my view, the quality of speaking the truth is above all these; it leads one to salvation, which is the ultimate aim of life. It is the quality that eases our goals at all aspect.

iii. **Supervening**. It guides our lives through which we get the essence of our personality, that is, what functions humans have to perform for better living. Supervening, by nature, are the obstacles that arise while doing any task, but we do not know when it happens. They happen all of a sudden when one is not aware of such types of situations. It is asserted that any global, national, or local problem may be solved through the practical application of human values in our society. So, the act of humanity is considered to be the highest value in global society, which can be achieved by keeping into consideration the preservation of the historical, ethical, cultural and distinctiveness of nations, states and communities. We can ensure human unity among all castes and creeds by adopting acts that can only be recognized by human values such as truth, kindness, benevolence, peace, love, dignity, respect, forgiveness, etc. Our action must be based on universally accepted values, because it is human values that are to be treated as the keys to solving any problem. In our ancient (Vedic) literature, the word value is denoted by the word “Artha” which means “the source of the livelihood, that is, the persons engaged in various occupations to maintain the livelihood”. Therefore, values play a great role in sustaining the culture and heritage of any society; they prove to be a source of prosperity for any nation, so it becomes a necessity to study the subject, that is, value education. Cleanliness and development are indicators of the prosperity and economic condition of the inhabitants, which in turn reflect the existence of value education in that society. The study reveals that providing value education to the people means adding virtues to their activities; it is the simplest and most effective procedure to raise the values of the masses and it also keeps society strong socially, politically and economically, resulting to a healthy society.

CHAPTER - 2

Objective

The objective of the study is to understand the concept of "duty up to rightful act." This concept highlights that values can inspire individuals to lead a righteous life and have a significant impact on our daily lives. It provides us with a sense that we are leading an enlightened life by teaching us about living standards and enhancing our capacity and thoughts for the right purpose. Therefore, it becomes our responsibility to properly apply these concepts before taking any action. Consequently, the study of value education should be made compulsory for children right from the beginning of their schooling. This will contribute to the establishment of a healthy society, leading to better living and should be the ultimate aim of humanity.

According to our ancient scriptures, the education on value properties, whether they are individual, social, national, or international, is based on the principles of human values. It is the task of moral and social theory to find a set of laws that possess three fundamental properties:

1. Stability, which implies resistance to change. In the context of human values, this can be related to one's character, which should remain un swayed by deterioration under all circumstances. It is observed that value properties tend to be more stable, especially in women who are more conservative and have not forgotten the habit of

benevolence toward helping the needy. A firm character in a person keeps them stable in all aspects, making them more perfect and reliable.

2. Behavior is the way a person or thing acts or reacts, so it is a function of the person's characteristics and his life experiences. It is observed that behavior may be observed directly or indirectly; direct behavior is physical behavior that can be studied by its actions, whereas indirect observations require a decision-making process. Human behavior is very unpredictable; it is classified as:

   i. **Caused Behavior**. Caused behavior is that behavior by which some effects are being observed by one's action and the element of one's action have the intrinsic properties of the behavioral events.

   ii. **Motivated Behavior**. Motivated behavior is that which activates one's willingness to exert efforts for the accomplishment of the desired target. It is the inner state of one's mind that prepares gets ready one's behavior to imply the committed target. So, motivation keeps the team working responsibly, effectively and efficiently to complete the committed task. The only thing that is to be observed is that, a leader must be a good motivator.

   iii. **Goal-oriented** behavior means achieving the committed goals with discipline and in time. Albert Einstein said "If we want to live a happy life, tie ourselves to a goal, not to people or things." Setting the goal means setting any event to such an extent that success may happens without fail. It is the quality in human beings that never lets one's off, as everyone wants success in life, but it is observed that all did not reach at the destination, which is due to the varying capabilities in each of us. So, to sum up this, it is education that puts one's to such a state that we too can call that person a goal-oriented behavioral person, it is a way of life we must opt it to live such an ideal life. It is understood that a person acts according to his needs, it is observed that as one's needs get fulfilled, other needs get started and one acts as per that need. We are astonished to know that it becomes a continuous and unending process; moreover, from the above classification, we come to the conclusion that the behavior of a person becomes a dependent factor. So, this way by understanding the needs of a person, we can regulate their behavior, allowing us to accomplish our task very easily by fulfilling their needs.

It is also asserted that behavior is a hereditary phenomenon but circumstances make individuals to move slightly to the left or right, though not to the extent of deteriorating their character. This is because individuals have adopted the demands of society. In conclusion, good behavior consists of virtuous actions that are appreciated and admired by everyone.

3. Ultimate human satisfaction: Indian culture is very vast in terms of linguistics, logistics and education, where everyone has the freedom to act as per his own accord but it must be in discipline. Someone feels satisfied with simple living, someone feels satisfied with materialistic living, someone feels satisfied with spiritual living and it may be more important to keep in mind that where one gets more satisfied, that is, satisfaction to such an extent that it does not harm anyone. But the ultimate satisfaction, in my view, is a knowledgeable living where one feels that whatever one does, there must be a virtuous act and how it gets viewed is when one starts living by heart, that is, when one lives with the God as the heart is the abode of God. It is possible only when the education that we possesses gets

> delivered in a systematic influence upon capable persons and the capable persons may influence this upon immature persons through instructions, discipline and harmony. This puts us in a reflection of the intellectual and social power of human beings. The knowledge of human values is the real education and must be developed among each individual. India is a value-based country where respect for truth, parents, elders and authority is considered a prime duty of a human being. This leads to a civilized society, as Indian history reavels.

In our system, the system that runs our lives, the values are the intrinsic worth of something and in our beliefs, we consider this worth to be a good one. The good may be a matter of someone's opinion or taste of someone's, or it may be driven by ethos, culture, creed, etc. and it is observed that all values are relative to each other, except the value of life. Life is universal and objective; our life is for a dual purpose; we live for our own values and we think good of others too. So, it means values denote the worth of someone or something; everyone has credential aspects of value of their own accord; living as well as non-living have their values, which are judged by others according to their characteristics. So, value is defined as the "intrinsic worth of living as well as non-living bodies." Values reflect the intrinsic and extrinsic behavior of the entity in each subject, which we perform daily or for future planning for survival or innovation. Ethical values are sometimes used synonymously with values, which we use synonymously with goodness, which should be the aim of life. It is asserted that the importance of values is utmost necessary for humans to lead a peaceful life and ultimately for human satisfaction. We must go to our oldest scripture, which is the Vedas, which is a trove of knowledge in all aspects. Let us consider some aspects that play a role in our daily lives and prove useful for healthy living.

CHAPTER - 3

System

Y<ins>**oga Study**</ins>. Yoga is not simply a study but a science of human life; it is a study of a human's mental, physical and social states, conforming to improved health, less greed and efficient management of one's life. The Yogic way of life is the best prescription of cashless medicines with a cent percent recovery rate; it is provided by our saints with their great research work on living life. It imparts real education for maintaining sound human health and values in order to live a peaceful life. It leads one to wisdom and proper spiritual development that make one understand the real value of humans. It trains one for the right attitude and human values, is a symbol of evaluating human health and is a process of value education. It is the science at every age of life for promoting human values for social peace. Its literature suggests that to enrich our values, we must read holy books, listen to saint's lectures, accompany collective prayers, etc., which makes us fearless and God-fearing. Nature is beautiful; beauty is the value of nature, which everybody too likes; it is a value like truth and goodness because it is an aspect of reality and well worth human's quest for it. The man feels himself imperfect without this and it remains a quest in human beings to attain perfection, which is due to the characteristics of the human's mind since ages. Our great Rishi Manu's literature has views on human values, which are as follows: The Manu literature, also known as Manav duty literature, is the oldest analytical text and is classified as the most authoritative as it contains the duties prescribed by God. It consists of teaching and preaching human values. The great Rishi presented a comprehensive and outstanding sociological work for society and its impact on society, reflecting the wisdom of ancient India. The main objective of this work is that we must move away from all castes and creeds while evaluating human values and focusing on the knowledge of education. A group of social systems assumes that wealth is evil, but our scholar (Rishis) narrates that this is a very good instrument for judging humans' attitudes, so wealth is neither evil nor the greatest good but simply an essential instrument for human living. So, everything has two aspects: one good and one bad. We have to choose which one should be adopted to live a valuable life.

Human values, as per Vedic literature, give us the vision of living in oneness, according to which it is understood that we always struggle in multiple areas to sustain life. To make it a success for an individual or society as a whole, it depends on analytically assessing the problems of the day and the timely course of action that makes us capable of building healthy and holistic societies. These are universal truths that inspire humanity to do research work to rise higher and for perfection, which we can acquire through meditation and education. This increases our consciousness inwardly and outwardly and maintains flow in our body system, which our scriptures have given the name of "self-attainment" which is the ultimate "absolute value". Mahatma Vidur, one of the prominent philosophers who wrote "Niti literature," was also a good orator. According to their literature, the human values in one's life are those in which one has knowledge of the customs of different countries but never exults at his own happiness nor delights in another's misery. A person who does not repent after giving charity is said to be a man of good nature and conduct. Vidur teachings are a guide to all of us, to rulers, to the general public and to ascetics and text as follows:

i. The man who thinks for self-interest only, the cruel and heartless one.
ii. The highest good is righteousness, which leads to salvation. Forgiveness is the only way to peace; knowledge is the only way to give contentment and benevolence and non-violence is the only way to give happiness.
iii. The way to remain happier is for those who have power but are persuaded with forgiveness and for those who are poor, running a charity.
iv. Lust, anger and greed are the way to hell.
v. One should avoid consulting these four types of people, viz., foolish people, people who are slow in their actions, who are thoughtless and who are flatterers.
vi. These five persons should be worshiped with respect, viz., father, mother, fire, soul and teacher.
vii. These six faults should be avoided to attain prosperity and happiness, viz., sleep, drowsiness, fear, anger, laziness and procrastination.
viii. We must abstain from such acts, viz., adultery with other women, dice, hunting, consuming alcohol, harshness of speech, severity of punishment and misuse of wealth, as all these lead to calamity.
ix. The acts that are indications of destruction are, viz., hating the saints, arguing with saints, appropriating saint's possessions, taking the life of a saint, taking pleasure in revealing saints and not providing any help when they ask for something.

The one who admits his fault without renouncing it by others and feels ashamed becomes the preceptor of the whole world and gets great honor. This shows that the Vidur Niti commences with "to whom sleep evades" and "the characteristics of wise men and the traits of foolish persons", Mahatma Vidur spread a wide spectrum of varied rules of conduct satisfying all walks of life at all times, even though at present the degradation of human values is rampant in the whole world.

Chanakya Niti (350–275 BCE), popularly known as Vishnu Gupta or Kautilya, was a great philosopher, economist, teacher and his texts are filled with lots of life lessons. According to history, he got his education from Takshashila University, an ancient university of the Great Bharat. He was prime minister under the reign of Chandragupta Maurya (321-297 BCE), founder of the Mauryan Empire (322–185 BCE). His guidance took the Maurya Empire to the territory right from modern Iran to almost the whole Indian subcontinent, that is, the largest empire of all time. He documented his guidance, which proved to be successful in running a prosperous and valuable life. Some guidance are as follows:

i. The first and foremost quality in humans is that one must use one's education and knowledge in every aspect; education beats beauty and youth. Education is an endless learning system; it can be gained up to any limit without any fear of loss, whereas wealth has limits and is likely to be prone.

ii. Be cautious in making any decision. Three questions must be kept in mind while taking any undertaking: "whether it needs to be done, its outcome and its worth". It is very important to note that whatever we say or write or any decision we take, it has an impact not only on our lives but also on the integrity of others. So, if we wish to keep our lifestyle intact, we must follow these rules thoroughly.

iii. Wealth acquired through wrong means is a poison for one's success; the definition of this poison is that it tastes good initially but leaves one with nothing except a brutal end. So, one must have a passion for money and power, but not at the cost of one's values and principles.

iv. Humanity and humility lie in the service of elderly and old people; rendering honest service to sufferers is the true knowledge of humanity. Harsh and bitter words can cause irreparable loss, which can be more harmful than the pain from fire burns. So, we must speak politely and avoid speaking rudely, which hurts anyone.

v. Hard work is the key to success; a wise man saying and it is foolish people saying that luck is the key to success, one may ultimately ruin their lives in the wait of luck; it is a wrong practice. So, we must put our sincere and hard work efforts into the tasks that we have undertaken; it keeps us at our destination.

vi. Never insult a noble man, a wise man, or a teacher; the noble person should be treated with respect and due respect should be given for their wisdom. Our attitudes must be revealed by our actions, not by words, as actions speak louder than words.

vii. Greed is a sin; it keeps one's mind in one direction, that is, it leads one to insatiable desires and pollute one's mind for material gain. One's intellect fails to distinguish between right and wrong and gets adopted to unfair means to achieve the glittering desires, which ultimately leads to a vulnerable condition.

viii. **Arrogance**. Arrogance is our greatest enemy. A human is a social animal that lives in a society that, comprises people of different tastes and cultures, giving birth to different events that become the causes of our enjoyment and sorrow and sometimes they lead us to a prestige issue.

In such situations, we must act righteously with humility and never resort to arrogance. Real knowledge is when we have control over our senses and maintain harmonious relations with others at all times.

ix. Charity is the prime duty of everyone and should be performed humbly in a righteous manner and to the deserving. It gives satisfaction and happiness to our inner being.

x. Non-violence is the basic principle of all castes and creeds, as it leads us to peace of mind. So, we must approach all matters with peace and avoid violent means such as anger. We should have full control over our anger and never let it have control over us. Our mother is the best teacher of us, so it is our first and foremost duty to have respect for and care for our devotional act at all times. One's character is very well depicted in one's behavior and our values and morals are the reflection of our behaviors while dealing with others. Our true character is a reflection of our actions, that is, how much we have respect and ease for people who are marginally different from us. A good and strong character is when one remains firm in one's values and principles in all odd conditions. The values preserve the good quality status of a human's personality as it pertains to the moral standard that humans apply to human's societal activities; it is an enduring belief with such principles that it not only guides us but also puts us on an ideal level.

Values are the indicators of bodily matters, representing their worth in context to morally, economically and socially, which helps us in determining or choosing the best way of living and also leads us in applying the right course of action. As such, values reflect the image of the person. In short, value is an entity that is good, desirable and worthwhile. The essence of value is "equal rights for all", "excellence deserves admiration" and "people should be treated with respect and dignity". The values have a special status in all aspects and bear excellent expression in the human dimension. It is learned that the concept of values passes through the soul, which means that every interaction is unique and imminent. So, the study of values is so important that philosophers put their views as follows:

i. **Universal Values**. The universal values are those values, whose, worth and values remain the same for all people at all times, such as the knowledge of the Vedas, which endorses the uplift of humanity and entrusts upon all learned persons to preach for such a conducive environment where peace, progress and prosperity of mankind are the main agendas of life. So, we call the Vedas a knowledge of universal values. Vedic and Sanskrit literature are considered ideals of mankind as their scientific and universal values make it possible to sustain the life of a human being in all eras. Speaking the truth and taking actions that are associated with morals, non-violence, etc. are all examples of universal values. It may be good or bad, depending on its characteristics and as assessed by the people. It helps us to create the innovation through which we get experiences that make us helpful in serving society.

ii. **Human Values**. Humans have a diverse culture, so human values can be viewed in various aspects. Human values are the tools for managing human relations and an instrument for peace in conflicts; they proved to be positive and effective to humanity. Human value encompasses character, aesthetic preferences, human endeavor and social order. A brief view of all these aspects:

Character pertains to both living and non-living entities by which we can identify their status and may be valued accordingly. So, as we are studying its living aspects, it means we are considering human values. It is the quality in a human being that one wishes for the betterment of all by which one gets betterment, which makes a human distinct from others. It especially refers to the moral quality of an individual, which indicates the disciplines in one's actions that sets one's status as an ideal one. Therefore, the character of a human being has a distinguishing effect on others; it bears the value of the human.

Aesthetic preferences are art, beauty, enjoyment, or taste. The diverse culture of humans shows his capability for preserving the beauty of nature through the concept of his art; old monuments are examples of human art. Conserving nature means saving the lives of all creatures on this planet, which is a prime virtue and must be our objective. It shows that the nature of humans is not to harm anyone. It adds to human values.

Human endeavor means striving for morality in our actions. It is asserted that morality is derived from education, so education is a human endeavor. It is education that makes our lives purposeful, to serve humanity. Therefore, human endeavor is toward education, as it is only education that keeps humans in the right direction and makes them distinctive from others; that is, it makes us valuable.

Social order pertains to human society, which is associated with human values and their importance in human society. So, the social orders are assumed to be a text of developed ideas, beliefs and patterns of conduct and feelings, which proved to be useful as it guides to human conduct and for managing human society. It is being observed and a well-known fact that human values are facing a crisis of survival in modern society. In spite of all these, it is again a fact that these are the human values that have saved mankind. The materialistic world has made humans self-centered, that is, selfish, by which the birth of various problems has taken place, such as nuclear families, where one forgets their next blood relations in the passion of a good job and there is nobody who stands in favor of them in hard times and it is certain that there are more hard times in life than good times, which should be kept in consideration for all. It is believed that the solution to all problems may be found through the practical application of human values, because human values may be treated as a key to solving any problem. Our actions must follow global and universally accepted values, which may help us reduce the problems caused by the ego of humans.

iii. **Personal Values** provide the internal quality of the individual, such as good, beautiful, desirable, constructive, useful, etc. It is the characteristics and behavior of an individual that are the driving force behind one's personality and actions and by which the value of an individual can be assessed. The values of an individual help in generating one's life goals, guide us in difficult situations, increase our self-confidence, reflect our choices and help us understand the internal quality of an individual. It is observed that an individual possesses six internal values and three external values; internal values are self-respect, a warm relationship, a sense of accomplishment, self-fulfillment, fun, enjoyment and excitement; external values are a sense of belonging, being well respected and security. All these values are important and a necessity of life and are due to one's interpersonal relationships and personal and non-personal factors.

iv. **Cultural Values**, the important aspects of culture, are that they guide us through societal norms and beliefs, the values which are generally not transmitted or diffused from parents to children, it is seen in some cases that children get affected and a change in their attitude is noticed, Though, their parents have a well-cultured indentity. It is observed to some extent that this happened where intercultural relations may have developed, which may be due to certain factors such as environmental, incidental, etc. Parents of different cultures have different values that affect the beliefs and attitudes among their children. For example, it is observed that college students who are entering a maturing stage show more interest in their personal well-being than in the welfare of others. This shows that a change in the system of values has taken place, which is a serious threat to humanity, though institutions are creating the environment to bring a balance between humanity and inhumanity to generate a conducive culture. Culture can be broadly classified as: individual culture, shared by family or by close associates of a family, has its values among its close members only; then there is societal culture, which has its values as per the respect and honor received by other groups; then there is status culture, the values one got as per the honorarium one received or the chair one held; then there are moral values, which are above all, that is, morality is life. It is a sin if politics is done without principles, so we must learn moral education, which imparts values like democracy and justice, as it is a field where we can develop our morality and values. Values are generally received through culture; every culture has its own norms and values; therefore, different cultures have different levels of values. So, culture has a profound influence on the psychology of individuals and on the social structure, where humans have interactions and a source of identification. It becomes necessary that the basics of value be clarified, whereas value clarification consists of" what is the purpose of our life and what is the worth of our work?" It encourages us to define our own values. Since ancient human life was simple and pure and itself an incredible one, it reflects the purpose of our life, which the human considers to be: Firstly, the human's actions must be an ideal that suits all except the violators; secondly, the human must help the needy accordingly; as such, it makes us valuable. Because, the worth of our work is only recognized by others, so our credit or discredit depends on the judgment of others and it should be, as one's is always right, which should not be and a mandatory wrong. But it is seen that, our actions are our recognition, which makes us capable of assessing the value of our actions and also helps in understanding the values of others too. The culture of India is very complex but rich in values, so there is unity in diversity; it is the strength of India. In India, we respect the society as it is believed that everyone in the society is doing one's assigned task orderly, but there is one more philosophy where the individual and society are viewed as two complementary and incomplete entities, tied to a relationship of ensuring the well-being of all, which our ancient culture reflects. But it is observed in some cases that those who are controllers of society or who have given this concept are generally violators of the law. So, there becomes a necessity of enforcement of legal laws to keep the functioning of the society in proper order, whereas we must view the society as the future of the nation and emphasis is put on keeping the society from a moral perspective. This leads us to a vision of righteousness by which we can expect a better society, as in Indian culture morality is considered above the legal implications. Touching the feet of elders shows great respect for elders. It is believed that elders bestowed blessings on younger people for their long lives and happiness and it happened. Namaste, the gesture of the Namaste, is part of Indian culture; in Sanskrit, its meaning is "I bow to you," which means the divine in me bows to the divine in you. It is being practiced during meetings and greetings with each other and also has the spiritual significance of putting himself as egoless in the presence of others, that is, paying respect to others; moreover, meeting the palm means we honor the God in the person to whom we are meeting. It is more than the words and its gestures and it gets suited to all ages, right from young to old, friends to strangers. Placing the two palms together and bowing the head slightly toward the meeting one are such gracious moments that they extend friendship in love, respect and humility. Atithi Devo Bhava means guests are considered equal to God and people feel happy when any guest comes to their home. Due respect and the utmost care are the priorities generally to be followed in honor of the guest.

v. **Relative values or Absolute Values**. The study suggests that there should be a precise definition of values or what is the measure of them. Value comprises ethics, which means value associated with morality; we measure it as the value of aesthetics and in economics, it is the quantitative measure of utility. It is asserted that ethics and aesthetics confirm the tendency toward goodness, with the view that all value determinations are based on aesthetic judgments. The judgment is free, independent and detached from any desires or emotions; it is asserted that each single value existed only for a definite subject at a definite time. It is noted that valuable stimuli have a sensation of priority, whereas we are unaware of whether the sensation is based on relative or absolute values. Therefore, we ascertain the relative or absolute values independently by using modified set norms identified for living and non-living entities. Absolute values are values compared with the absolute standard; absolute values are true values that do not change, whereas relative values are formed when compared with other values. In order to clarify it, take the Celsius and Kelvin scales. In the Celsius scale, freezing and boiling points are 0 and 100 degrees, whereas in the

Kelvin scale they are 273 and 373 degrees. 0 of Celsius is equal to 273 of Kelvin and Kelvin is an absolute value of 273 with respect to the absolute value of 0 of Celsius. So, temperature, when stated in degrees Kelvin, has an absolute value of 273, because it is with respect to the absolute zero of Celsius. Relative value exists in relation to or in proportion to something else; it is part of the universe and exists in relation to the whole. Let us consider the goodness of the person in relation to other entities. A person is well-known for their attitudes and character. Attitudes reflect a person's emotions, beliefs and behavior toward a particular person, object, or thing. Attitudes whose actions proved useful and had an impact on our daily lives are known as attitude strength. It guides our actions and also gives us a sense of evaluating the quality of a person. Character: we generally read that one has lost his influence and power due to one's action and may have faced criminal proceedings. This is due to the fact that one lacks one quality, that is, the quality of character, which is such a moral force that is both effective and enduring. Both are virtues and a good source for determining the relative value of a person in contrast to attitude and character. An old saying says that a wise man is one who knows the relative value of things.

vi. **Intrinsic or Extrinsic Values**. The dictionary meaning of intrinsic is belonging to the essential nature of things, that is, the value of the things needs no justification, whereas extrinsic values are those that are not part of the essential nature, that is, the value of the things needs justification by other values to operate. The philosopher asserted that intrinsic value plays a foundational role upon which other values make a reference for their justification to implement. Some entities deserve good for themselves and provide good for others too, such as science. Understanding science proved to be good for itself and a means of achieving other goods. In such cases, the sum of the instrumental value and intrinsic value of an object may be considered when putting the same in a value system, which is a set of consistent values and measures. The philosopher asserted that the value of any entity depends either on its own worth or its relationship with something else, that is, on its worth. A human, by its nature, is analytic in all aspects, which makes an individual a successful one. For example, suppose I have a business shop, for which I get a job. The time spent on this work puts one's reward in the form of money, which leads to a fulfilling life. So, to evaluate these events, we need no justification, that is, the consequences of the events are right or the events are self-explanatory, the values as per the circumstances or moral judgment. These are called intrinsic values. For example, suppose I want to sell the shop. The value that I wish to desire needs the justification of value by some other appropriate means, that is, to justify the desired value. This is an extrinsic value. By value, a good, a commitment, an ideal, or a principle are such interests that one not only cares about them but also endorses or assents to such caring where one understands the sanctity of the value or wherever it feels necessitated. Three aspects are to be considered while ascertaining the values of any entity: ethical theories, theories of the good and theories of value. Ethical theory endorses right and wrong actions and their reasons and also considers the relationship between rightness and goodness. It endorses the principle of morality, which prescribes what human character and conduct should be in aspects of obligations such as rights, rules, fairness, benefit to societies, etc. Theories of the good ask only about the good; they tell us what is actually good, what is not and why, all of which are included in the theories of goods. Theories of value justification justify the good with relevance and circumstances.

vii. **Positive and Negative Values**. Values that drive us to virtue are positive values, Aristotle condensed them into one word "good". Truth, goodness and beauty are such words that influence and motivate us to take the right actions, their outcome is happiness, which leads us to positive values. Positive values yield positive behavior, that is, our interactions with others are relevant, which yields good relations, which means positivity in all aspects. So, positivity is a force that puts us in a state where we feel everything in a pleasant manner. Therefore, it becomes advisable to think on the positive side of everything and it is a good quality to find positivity in everything, it makes us capable of adopting ethics in our speech, deeds and thoughts. Where there is positivity, it is obvious that negativity also exists there. Negative is the opposite of positive, so the ability to think or observe on the negative side of something is called negativity. It results in a lack of peace, prosperity and confidence. Any action, whether it leads to happiness or suffering, yields anti-value or negative value, unpleasantness, harm and the concept of disintegration of the people. It is observed that there exist positive and negative aspects in all entities, both are forces that exist in everyone and affect one's life, one has to remain active with both. The extract is this that how negativity can be utilized to act as positivity. In some situations, by speaking a lie, it may act as a good one. Though it has negative aspects, such as saving the life of someone, which is considered the highest virtue, we must accept such an occasion, but in the long run, it's better to stay positive with life and discard negativity to enhance the quality of life.

viii. **Protected Values** are the values to whom we keep trade-offs, as these are the values that are absolute for us. The human being himself is a better judge and takes decisions accordingly to maintain the sanctity of the human. We used to strive with our values to decide on the right path, feel satisfied when we acted in accordance with our values and feel more satisfied when we knew that what we had done was right for us. We feel inconvenient when we do not act according to our values, as values are the credits of our work that are identified by others and are known to be "values." It means our values have an impact on deciding the direction of our lives and these are the values that, by following, we get a sense of idealism and a valuable one. People with these protected values take one's life as an absolute and a sacrifice for an individual, as we have not to compromise it for any benefit that may erode our value. Secondly, it encourages us to accept the consequences that may have developed in lieu of these values. These protected values often contain moral or ethical undertones and are generally interrelated, as the value of the divine has the value of preeminence, the value of integrity and the value of family. Everybody has their own beliefs and views in this context. My beliefs and views are as follows: My belief in a divine being as I value God above all values, as God is omnipotent and our existence is by Him, keeping God above all is a justified dialogue. Whatever I am having or whatever I was having is all by His grace, that is, by adopting His lessons, all this good has happened; therefore, this is not something to be traded; therefore, my conscious is firm, not to compromise my values in lieu of any benefits and to keep all time regards for the Almighty. Therefore, God has become a protected value for me and I will sacrifice all that I have for Him. The value of integrity is the character of a person related to that person's moral values and behavior. From its very meaning, it is "united not to be divided", that is, one is firm with his values, not compromising at any cost; it reflects the moral quality of a person. The person's integrity can be judged as:

a. His acts toward wholeness and coherence
b. Professional responsibility
c. Moral reflections
d. Values like incorruptibility and impartiality
e. Laws and rules
f. Moral values and norms
g. Honesty
h. Exemplary behavior

Example: suppose I purchased an article costing Rs. 200, but erroneously, the incumbent returned me Rs. 400 in exchange for Rs. 500.It's now my moral duty that I should not exchange my integrity for petty financial benefit and get that cleared from the incumbent. I believe in righteous works, so, such things can't be trade-offs, so, I value integrity. The value of family, every family has values and in some cases the family is known by the values that family keeps. It is generally observed that every family tries to maintain a harmonious culture that exhibits a valued family. Everybody wants that the growth of his children should be an ideal one and this becomes possible when parents practice virtues, the same being followed by the children. So, if one wants that his children don't smoke, then one has to quit that so that his children may follow that accordingly. It is the parents who have to decide which is better for their family and may prove to be a valued family. This creates respect in children for their parents, which adds social values to the family. In this way, a bond is being established in the family where everyone cares for everyone and a valued family is recognized in society. So, I have a high regard for my family. I place high value on my family. It is very difficult to resolve conflicts when competition comes into play.

CHAPTER - 4

Philosophy

V**alue System**. A value system is a set of consistent thoughts that refer to human integrity. Everyone is unique in their own accord and gives weightage and preference to values as per their own. So, when two individuals or groups show different consent for the same value in question, it is said that these individuals have different value systems. Even though they may share common views on many values, this disparity in their value systems leads to conflicts, pushing them to disagree on certain matters, regardless of the rightness or wrongness of the case. In essence, a moral system is a set of moral codes authorized by the competent authority to exercise it for the welfare of society, mostly concerning the field of ethical and ideological value systems. The ethical value system distinguishes between good and bad, right and wrong and moral and immoral, whereas the ideological value system deals with politics, economics, caste and creed and social norms.

Value systems are categorized as personal or societal. Personal value systems are held by an individual and are applicable only to that individual, while societal value systems are held by a community or society and apply to the entire community or society. Communal value systems are governed by legal codes. They can be internally consistent, meaning they have a high degree of internal consistency, which implies that a measure yields the same result each time it is undertaken. Values that do not contradict each other are considered inconsistent. Ideally, a value system ought to be consistent.

Value systems can be categorized as idealized or realized. Idealized value systems are absolute and have no exceptions. The values are codified as a strict set of texts on the pretext of morality and behavior. Realized values contain exceptions to resolve the contradictions between the ideal values and practical realities in everyday circumstances.

Exceptions are the rules used to resolve contradictions between values and practical circumstances. These exceptions can be categorized as abstract exceptions, which are applicable in all situations and situational exceptions, which are specific to certain situations. Exceptions prove to be useful for defining a consistent value system and help us to prioritize values. For example, killing a person is considered the gravest sin, but in war, killing an opponent soldier is a matter of pride, as it saves one's own life. Otherwise, the opponent would kill them. Taking a defensive strategy in such a situation is not a sin. Therefore, it is asserted that our formal value system (idealized or realized), which is associated with default exceptions, is assumed to be good unless or until a high-priority value is violated.

A value system whose exceptions are abstract and generalized enough to be used in all situations is said to be an internally consistent value system, whereas a value system whose exceptions are highly situational or whose exceptions are inconsistently applied is said to be internally inconsistent. Example: truth is above all and has high positive values. We received this concept from our ancestral, texts and a universal fact. But in some situations, lying is not wrong. If someone saves one's life, lying may not be wrong. Let there be a Boucher who is running after the calf to kill him and one meets him at a four-way crossing from where the calf runs. The Boucher asks that one, have you seen the calf and in which direction the calf went? The person who saw everything tells a lie and misguides the Boucher. So, this lie is not wrong and one did a specific thing at a specific time. This comes under the category of a situational exception because saving one's life is highly valuable. Conflict value system.

Values are the sources that encourage people to maintain positive bonds with others, resulting in a harmonious environment in society. Values are the beliefs; they put the people in a disciplined life and make them understand to differentiate between good and bad, right and wrong, just and unjust. Value disputes arise only when there are incompatibility conditions, when one tries to enforce one set of values on others, or when there is a value system that does not allow for divergent beliefs. In search of right, it is very evident that one has a contradiction with the other, as one's view does not tally with others, but there are certain universal truths to whom one has to accept, keeping into consideration the reference point where one side is right and the other is disobeying it. It is observed that there are still some people who put their views contradictory to logic, to whom we may call it value conflicts, which may be viewed as: one's knowledge and capability to deal with conflicts can result in conflicts, differing expectations lead to conflicts, assumptions lead to conflicts; putting value as per one's own convenience leads to conflicts; growing up in different cultures leads to value conflicts; and there may be more. These may be classified as:

i. **Intrapersonal Conflicts and Interpersonal Conflicts**. Intrapersonal conflicts are due to one's individual thinking; if it does not tally with others thoughts, it leads to restlessness and uneasiness and sometimes leads to depression. These conflicts involve the psychological involvement of one's thoughts, values, emotions and principles, which occurs within an individual. Interpersonal conflicts: these conflicts occur between two individuals. This is due to variant choices among people, which result in incompatible opinions, thus resulting in conflicts.

ii. **Intragroup Conflicts and Intergroup Conflicts**. Intragroup conflicts are a type of conflict that arises among individuals within a group. Incompatibility and misunderstanding among the individuals are the causes of such conflicts. Intergroup conflicts take place when misunderstandings arise among different groups within the organization due to the varied set of goals and interests of these different groups.

Conflict is an inevitable part of life; we all have our own ideas and views according to our capabilities. The most interesting thing is that everyone is of the opinion that my idea is the right one and must be enforced, whereas it is to be noted that enforcement is based on values, not on words, which puts each of us in conflict. The conflicts are not always negative, but they are a good source of innovation. The very important thing is to always try to avoid wasteful and damaging conflicts and even then, if they happen, try to keep them to a minimum.

Veda and Value Systems. It is asserted that our planet is as old as the creation of the universe and so is the history of humans. A human who is dependent on nature tries to explore himself by constraining himself within the limits of nature, as we know that exceeding the limits means deteriorating the environment, which in turn affects the life of the human. Therefore, to protect nature is humans' first and foremost duty, as it keeps us surviving. India is such a subcontinent where we find the oldest scripture, which has a literature on value-based living. These value-based scriptures have influenced us in every aspect of our lives. It is learned that the Government of India formed a committee on value education in 1999, in which they identified five core universal values, which are:

a. Truth
b. Righteous conduct
c. Peace
d. Love
e. Non-violence

These values are very much described in these old scriptures, depicting their effects on human characteristics. The Vedas, the old and sacred scripture of the world, are a composite text on the way of life by which one can ascertain the culture and philosophy of humanity. The literature asserts that "value-based living is a living with the divine," so it becomes necessary for us to live a life that should be possessed with values. The Vedas, which lay emphasis on right conduct, which acts as a base of development for the personality of the individual, add value and should be taken as an asset of the individual. The Vedas have an immense influence on Indian society and have divided this creation into human and nature (purusha and prakriti). Purusha is very much connected to purushartha, that is, where there is human, there are actions and a core source of the Indian value system.

According to this belief, humans are supreme and have influence in all directions and in all beings. It is that supreme self that exists in all beings and has the reasons and objectives for our existence on this planet. In my view, the reasons for our existence on this planet are a big task. Firstly, our duty is to conserve nature, which has a major role in providing existence to us. As the soul needs a body to abode, the body needs energy to survive, which our planet makes sure to provide, that is, adequate availability of water, air, earth, fire and sky. These are the basics for survival. Secondly, our duty is to keep the message of God alive, which is available by virtue of the Vedas, that is, not to harm anyone and to communicate it person to person so that everyone shall be well aware of consequences before committing any violation and let virtue prevail everywhere. Thirdly, everyone wants to remain active in his prescribed mode, so it remains with God, that is, maintaining the accounts of humans, as humans have to be treated as per one's Karma, which varies for everyone. To keep the accounts and to provide justice to everyone is not a simple matter; it is believed that whatever happens, it is as per the will of God and as per our Karma; moreover, it puts us in faith in God that whatever happens in our lives is for our betterment and a reward of our Karma. In this way, everyone remains busy at their own accord, the universe gets activated and we call it the law of nature. So, if you trust God and do the right thing, everything will get right. The objective of purushartha is mankind, which is the highest goal in man's life to achieve. As it leads to a valued life, it has four functions.

1. **Righteousness**. Our every action should be right, purposeful and not damaging to anyone.
2. **Objectives** should be clear and common; the acquisition of wealth is the second most important objective of life and has the following forms

    i. **Knowledge**, which is the greatest wealth and has no fear of theft; both material and spiritual knowledge have an immense role in the lives of humans and are necessary to live and to keep pace with society.

    ii. **Health** is wealth, an old saying, so we must pay proper attention to our health so that, we can work physically, emotionally and mentally properly. It requires a sincere effort.

    iii. **Contentment** is also one of the forms of wealth. As contentment is happiness, it leads us to be honest and gives us patience to live with the available resources and circumstances.

iv. **Material Wealth**, is a wealth liked by everyone, which is a sin, so, it should be earned as per norms by which life may run smoothly. It is advisable that some portion of wealth be kept for benevolence, which must be a habit, it puts one's to help the needy.

3. Desires and pursuits, humans for development, but one should not be so after these, that it may create trouble for others, which is unethical. So, try to be content, as desires have no ends.
4. Salvation or liberation must be the goal of life, as everyone wants liberation, but very few reach it at such a stage, as everyone says it is difficult to reach at such a stage. But it is not difficult, it comprises two terms, firstly, it is the detachment, that is, one has to keep himself out from worldly affairs and second is one's commitment to liberation. It puts one's to liberate from misery and pain and puts them on the stage of "Ananda," where one feels himself with God. It is asserted that humans are an image of God, so, whenever one thinks it is the right time for him one must pursue these functions to fulfill the goal of life.

These functions lead us to a valued life, as they are interdependent and should be practiced as a whole by which we can realize ourselves. The exclusive pursuit of these creates balance in life and puts us at the destination. The Vedas put emphasis on morality and universalities, morality gives us a way of life, that is, to follow ethics, attitude, etc., whereas universality implies a value that we consider common for all, applicable for all and an example for all, such as mankind, peace, freedom, etc. It implies the ethical and moral standards prescribed in the Vedic text; it puts us in a harmonious and disciplined state of living, so we come to the conclusion that universal values and human values are co-related to each other. The Vedic literature, which is prevalent in the whole world, makes its maximum appearance in India and the follower of this puts ancient India at the apex in the field of civilization, culture and heritage. By virtue of it, the whole world gets influenced as it is based on scientific knowledge, by which the world emerges as a literary being, as the Vedas have a concept of "Vasudeva Kutumbkam," that is, the whole world is one family of God. This proved to be a universal fact and the literary fraternity of the world asserted and recommended that the Vedas are the oldest and visionary text of the world, written in the oldest language, which is Sanskrit. It is pertinent to say that it is such an analysis-based language that the computer has accepted this language in complete, whereas the rest of the languages are only partially accepted by the computer. It is asserted that the oldest civilization was the Indus Sarasvati River Valley civilization, which exists in India and is popularly known as the Vedic civilization. It is an example of people's contribution toward cultural and spiritual development, which is believed to be the hereditary of India. It means the people follow the rules and regulations of the Vedic scriptures, which put India at the apex of other civilizations. Therefore, it is asserted that the Vedas are from great India and by the Indian scientists (seers), whose vision was so great that people not only accepted the teaching of the Vedas in India but were followed by the whole world, which reflects the truthfulness of the literature. Shrimad Bhagavat Gita, our old scripture, is one of the solution providers to all our conceivable issues through its text; it is the ocean of wisdom where we find the knowledge of all disciplines. It emphasizes much on human values, where one has to maintain total renunciation for prohibited acts. As per scripture, the world is filled with wonderful opportunities, but for those who understand the sense of renunciation that keeps one's away from the attachment of worldly objects, it puts one's to a valued life. One must have control over anger, lust and greed, as these lead to the gate of hell and performing the duty as per scripture leads humans to the nature of truth, compassion, tranquility and non-violence. The Holy Gita preaches human values as follows:

i. One's senses and eyes should be impartial toward everyone and one should abstain from pretense.
ii. Actions and thoughts should be harmless to everyone and one should have an accommodating attitude.
iii. One should refrain from self-egoism and remain in a state of dispassion toward the objects of this materialistic world.

A human being keeps himself unique and there is no doubt about his uniqueness. Unfortunately, it is observed that whatever acts one does, one does with this attention that my actions are superior to others, which puts one's in a distinguished state, which is a mistake. As a human being there is no end to longing and struggles for objectives and desires; both are limitless. So, it keeps ourselves in a state of dispassion, we have to keep our minds in a state of contentment, not forcibly but through a commitment. By adopting the above-mentioned narrations, one's mind gets mastery over spontaneous thinking and gets fascinated with emerging situations, which helps us to deal with the problem effectively. This leads to a change in the attitude and ways of thinking of an individual and it also improves the efficiency of one's actions. These values enhance the quality of life, whatever one's activities may be. It is observed that if the business fraternity got these values adopted, it helped them achieve profitability, productivity and prosperity and it also helped the fraternity to become a disciplined. It adds value to the fraternity as well as to the individual. Moral human values are most important for mankind as they make us capable of solving some ridiculous practices that are prevalent in modern times, for which the biggest sufferer is the general public, such as competitive corruption. We should cut throat competition and put our effort on excessive consumerism; it puts the masses in their approach; it is a demand of the day and a good approach to the economy. The quality of human action is the quality of one's education, which in turn is the product of the culture and human values. Presently, it is time to inculcate ethical practices that keep ourselves in a healthy society. It is asserted that human and ethical values are the very foundation of our old scripture, with the view that they may bring about attitudinal change in a human's mind if these values are sincerely adopted and put to use in practice. As per scripture, it is asserted that an individual may move to three qualities, viz., Sattva, Rajas and Tamas; their importance in life is to keep society an ideal and not a miserable place where everyone has free access as per one's choice in the existence of discipline, the base of which is truth and honesty.

Sattva is pure and peaceful and has the power to illuminate self and others by way of one's action; it leads to happiness, virtue and knowledge.

Rajas lead to actions through attachments and activeness, resulting in wealth, fame and suffering. Tamas leads to idleness, sluggishness and ignorance. All these lead to the value system of an individual and are described in the text accordingly.

Sattvik Values. Actions that create non-violence, tolerance, mercy, contentment, truth, internal and external purity or cleanliness, steadfastness, everlasting and unconditional devotion toward the God, equanimity in both good and bad situations, approaching a bona fide spiritual teacher, modesty, humility, freedom from anger, renunciation, tranquility, aversion to fault finding, freedom from greed, gentleness, determination, vigor, forgiveness, fortitude, freedom from envy, surrender to the God, salvation, non-enviousness, satisfaction, dispassion, sincerity, faith, fearlessness, charity, controlling the mind, constantly seeking for eternal truth and austerity Such actions put one in the hands of a valued person and ultimately, this leads one to salvation, which is the ultimate aim of life and is adopted by noble persons.

Rajasik Values. actions that lead to greed, attachments, confusion, stinginess, pride, treachery, jealousy, vanity, expecting rewards and importance to wealth, power and status are said to be Rajasik values. These actions lead one to the materialistic world, where an individual happens to seek anxiety as one of the main sufferings. By the flow of wealth, one can get instant relief, which puts one to happiness, but his ill knowledge, not aware of this fact, puts one to a great sin, which ultimately leads to a miserable death. The people who are on the right path of life try to avoid such actions.

Tamasik Values. Actions that lead to malevolence, anger, deceit, obstinacy, arrogance, lust, ignorance, fear, laziness, procrastination, suspicion, delusion and aggressiveness are termed Tamasik values. It is observed in those people who always remain in fear and anxious and a source of such values; it is in those persons who by nature are law avoiders and have no planning to cast their duties; one must avoid such actions to keep himself a human being. The Vedas are the scriptures of knowledge, the other source of knowledge is education and it is education that puts us in a position of value and it is value that keeps the person in a position of distinction. Our ancient system of education is based on the Vedas and still we are following that, as it is so unique that the world's education system gets inspiration from it. It states that the system of delivering the education by the teacher and getting accepted by the pupil must be due honor and respect by the pupil to the teacher, such as bowing to the teacher before the start of the work, that it creates a bond of respect and affection between the teacher and the pupil, it develops a bond of morality among pupils. It proved to be a unique system of acquiring education; it makes the pupil disciplined, character-oriented in all aspects and a good source of innovation. There is no doubt that modern technology has a greater impact on our social lives, but our old system inspires us more if followed by our own traditional values. As per the scripture, it is asserted that at the time of convocation, the Indian scientists (Rishis) instructed their disciples about the moral duties to be followed and it is enjoined that one should never think of neglecting the Vedic studies and teachings. Knowledge, intelligence and spirituality have an important place in a human's life. In Indian society, the Vedas may be considered as their origin. In the Vedic ages, social, moral and spiritual values were considered the basis of development and reform in human life. The Vedic scientists (Rishis) who held moral, aesthetic and spiritual values are the results of their rigorous study in the realization of good, beauty and truth, which are eternal entities. Unity, integrity and self-confidence are the main discourses of Vedic traditions. The Vedas are very much related to Karman theory, which means the theory of one's actions or duty; that is, a human being is bound to maintain social responsibility toward all beings; thus, it signifies the duty and responsibility of a human for all his actions. As per scripture, every good action performed without any interest is covered under the term sacrifice, which means it directly relates to one's Karma. So, sacrifice is not a ritual, but a wide term that covers all good acts; it is the real way of life. It keeps us well aware of the living; its prime benefit is that it gets multitude, that is, it makes our future free from anxiety; secondly, the objective of sacrifice is for ethical development and for the welfare of society; this keeps us safe, guards the environment and maintains purity and peace in the body and mind of the individual.

The scripture suggests that we should work for universal unity, which means that there should be a culture of collective harmonious living. Such types of deeds are very much necessitated as the world is passing through a materialistic age that is, being assisted by the negativity of selfishness and the egoistic culture of the day. But it is in our curriculum right from the very beginning; that is, its roots are from the Vedas. The text prescribes that the teacher must insist that his pupil follow certain values throughout his life, such as speaking the truth. Values are necessary for rationalism, which brings peace and prosperity, so the objective of value is to uplift society in all aspects so that there prevails a conducive environment of positivity. It is the positivity of the literature that our Indian scientist (Rishis) established five thousand years earlier; it is expected, it may be older, but the written manuscript authentication available with the world is of this period. It endorses the scientific and traditionally value-oriented education system in all aspects; it keeps humans disciplined and responsible. The scripture suggests that humans are the best creation of the universe, possessing a sense of responsibility, being kind and being grateful toward everyone, as everyone is useful to nature and nature is life, so keep everyone important for life. Humans enjoy a sense of life by sharing and giving, which brings the ultimate happiness to our minds. The Vedas are such a treasure of knowledge that, it is very strange to note, that, how much old this knowledge came into existence, nobody knows, who is the writer, nobody knows, but how much modern it sounds and how this knowledge runs the whole world at every aspect put us to explore the system and ultimately we come to the conclusion that it is the Almighty who have created this and whatever is running, it is running according to His will, which is the abstract of Srimad Baghwat Gita, that is, "Karman philosophy," which states that one gets comforts and discomforts as per one's deeds, so, never be harmful to anyone. Therefore, to understand the context of the Vedas, it is very essential for us that we go through the teachings of the Vedas, which guide us at every step of our lives and enable us to sustain human life in this materialistic world. It is asserted that there exist different values in different people and, to a greater extent, in people of different cultures, so, keeping it more imperative, the values have been studied in various disciplines to maintain the sanctity of the subject.

CHAPTER - 5

Categories

Anthropology is a systematic study of humanity; it is the holistic study of people and cultures in the world, that is, what makes us human, which means studying the various aspects of human experiences. The subject values in question are very much connected with humanity, as humanity is by virtue of human values, so the study of anthropology gives us an opportunity to know about the ancient status of humans with regards to human values. It is the study of the past of humans in context to biological, social and archaeological activities, reflecting the nature of humans and making us capable of understanding and exploring their characteristics, showing what remains common in us and what makes us unique. Biologically, it refers to the study of humans' anatomy; it helps us to understand the similarities and differences among humans. It is very strange that there are more similarities than differences. It makes us capable of understanding the behavior of humans, which is an index of human values. Socially, it reflects the living of the human, that is, it shows that the human, who being fully equipped with basic amenities, means one has the capability to enjoy a prosperous life. It also reflects that there was no war as prosperity prevails here, it means there exists peace, which is the basics of human value. So, studying the social past of humans and comparing it with our present socio-cultural system makes us capable of understanding how much deterioration in our value system has taken place. Archaeology concerns over the objects reveals that human societies erected at that time are not available now, but certain monuments reflect the culture of that time. It is very helpful in understanding the nature of humans as art is a reflection of the mind. Studying all these helps us to evaluate the value system and lastly we opt for the best, which is the necessity of the time.

Axiology is the philosophy that studies the theory of values; it relates to ethics and aesthetics; ethics pertains to morals and principles (discussed earlier), whereas aesthetics relates to beauty, art, enjoyment, or taste. It means the quality of life which we call it the personality of the individual, that is, understanding the meaning of human values, that is virtue. Our ancient literature narrates this as:

We did not work at cross purposes but work for one purpose, which is the purpose of mankind, which makes our thoughts constructive, positive and creative. It makes our nation prosperous, that is, if a nation is prosperous, I am automatically prosperous; this must be our motivation. But it is asserted that the world has simply not been constituted by a number of variants but has been sustained by multi-level values without which it is impossible to characterize its social, political and spiritual aspects. All these multi-level values lead to self-preservation, that is, humans have become self-centered, keeping aside the vision of humor, by which such heinous problems arise that they become world problems, such as climate change, which is a creation of human's self-interest. This leads humans to live under the influence of many valued systems, it seems to be good, but ultimately makes the personality of humans devalued in real-life situations, as a person who is strong acts as per his convenience not as per norms, which leads humans to devalued. It is no one but only the human who has both the characteristics of selfishness and selflessness; this act is of selfish people who devalue the human.

Axiology is the study of multi-level values; its intrinsic feature, which is multidimensional and diverse, reveals that value is a complex multifactorial phenomenon as it has the symptoms of an inherent human attitude. It is observed and a fact that modern humans wish to adopt a multi-level value system where personal and global value becomes part of the human values as it helps the human being to keep pace with global society and consider it the only sustainable formation, but it is also being observed that, day by day, knowledge is approaching new horizons, so this also did not last long as Indians are very much connected with their inheritance, which keeps them to be in norms. The aim of the study is to coordinate the multi-valued world, that is, the personality of the human, in context to custom, tradition, culture, education and self-identification, which helps the individual in ascertaining the sustainable path. Lastly, the individual wants to switch over to that life, which gives the individual an ideal life. It is asserted that general human values always serve global ideals and its main aim is to preserve the planet Earth in its unique form by performing the universal norms, whereas we are witnessing the reverse of it, which is due to violations of norms. Everyone says that it should not be, but it is happening and the reason behind this is well-known by humans. It does not mean that we should stop working on innovations; rather, it gives us more strength to go deep into the subject so that we can put our attention to rectifying this evil. It is asserted that whatever was the value of an entity once, it was the personal value, as personal values are always conscientious and derived from life experiences, which latterly form the personal consciousness and get aligned with the object of life. Values are above the emotional reaction of an individual, while their valuable characteristics are the analysis of an axiological study. It is a real, active and prime theory that regulates the behavior of an individual. It has the background of the objective reasoning of human aspirations, orientation and activity, by which it acts as an integral part of the formation of a society, in general, for a social group and for the individual. The study reveals that the reliability of the study is directly related to human personality and the devaluation of values is by subjective origin, that is, by the decision of the human being. The transformation of values is an objective process that requires methodical analysis and is difficult to control by the personality. But the power of human personality lies in the cross-interaction of these processes. Therefore, personal and global values in close proximity to human values in the axiological sphere of the multivalued world which are capable of creating a fundamental and complementary system. Its interaction with identification that ensures the sustainability of the human personality and gets capable of restoring the integrity of the individual, the “self,” which was disrupted by the pace of modern life. Overcoming social segregation through the development and preservation of the diversity of the new communication forms comes to an authentication norm through the interaction of a multi-level value system.

The science and the values: It have been since decades that we considered science a systematic study of knowledge with evidence, but it is also free of values. The analysis suggests that in scientific activities, ethical values are to be considered the first and foremost priorities. It is asserted that science is based on facts, whereas values are the product of emotions, beliefs and experiences that have no scientific meaning. It does not mean that morality judgments are not applicable or not possible, but the reason is that value arguments don’t work as scientific arguments; it is the values that credit the work of science accordingly. The scientist explores the existence of values in science, as it is asserted that science is an epistemic and methodological process; it refers to a variety of things that occur, though they are related among themselves, but it is possible only if the process moves through norms, which mean that some directions are the accumulation of rights and the rights are the values of an entity under process. Science is the study of the universe, which needs exploration. Human beings are trying their best to explore and the change that we observe in our day-to-day is the advancement in technology. These are examples of this, but it is so unending that it puts human beings of not more than just a drop in the ocean. Science focuses exclusively on the natural world, which enables us to understand how the natural world works to sustain life on this planet. So, this unending task of the natural world cannot be run without norms, the results of which affect the millions of living and non-living species on this planet. So, to understand the value of science, the philosopher urged two theories: internalist and externalist. The internalist refers to analyzing the process from inside with regards to its education, cognitive methods and other values, which is a typical exercise of science. It does not reject the intervention of values with the reasons to achieve the goals, so consider it conditional, that is, on cognitive values. Cognitive values are the real source of scientific knowledge as they act as a basis for the research to be undertaken, which helps the scientist choose the most adequate way to achieve the goals. They also affect the scientific rationality that is based on this. Whereas the externalists considered this scientific task just like a human activity, the study evaluates the science in context socially, such as in view of the environment, biotechnology, cybernetics, etc. The scientist has a value system of their own accord, which is above emotions and beliefs, in favor of mankind and recognized by the scientific community. So, their value system does not coincide with modern societies and remains neutral to ethics.

Attitude and Values. Values are the guiding principles that ensure a virtuous life and enable the individual to seek right and wrong for the well-being of humanity. Whereas attitude represents the behavior of an individual possessing the capacity to dispose of something or someone, this varies as per the context and situation. These are attributes of human personality and are being discussed at the global level as ways to incorporate them into curricula to develop these terms using a variety of approaches as they prove to be a guiding instrument in the overall development of humans. There are some definitions and facts related to the concept of attitude and values that have proven beneficial for humans and society.

i. Aptitude refers to the natural capability of an individual; it makes one aware of the coming events and gets that disposition accordingly so that, one's actions run without interruption. One can achieve this by practicing the skill that, by natural capability, one has and the best way to assess this skill is self-evaluation. It may assess one's past and present, which helps in assessing the strengths and weaknesses in one's personality and may help to improve one's aptitude.

ii. Ethics and morality refer to norms and behavior, respectively. It puts us in such a state that we keep ourselves so conscious when taking any action that there should be no such acts that may harm anyone. So, these terms give us a valuable living.

iii. Social and emotional skills refer to the ability and capacity of an individual to interact with others; these terms proved to be successful in the development of humanity; positive responses are an indicator of a person's good attitude.

iv. Virtues are attributes of a person and are formed over time by having a habit of making the right responses, which is considered a valuable asset of a person who always has a mind for the betterment of humanity.

Studies show that paying respect and getting respect improves societal relations, which means that valuing others is the outcome of close relationships, which are essential for the development of communities. It also improves the academic outcome as the value of equality and social equity helps people understand their rights and responsibilities; it reduces inequality, which has divided communities, instead of integrity, which is essential for the survival of prosperity in the country. Justice is also associated with equality and is integral to individual and social well-being. Making judgments is very crucial for the judge, as one has to take into consideration the moral actions to protect the rights of others, as one is being a loser, so this is only done by adolescents who have a sense of justice and are associated with academic and social well-being. The international community has urged at the global level that these terms may be introduced in education curricula as they proved useful in helping students understand the meaning of integrity, which proved to be helpful in their future lives while interacting with social matters. It is asserted that this will ensure strength, renew trust in institutions among communities and develop and maintain values in citizens, such as respect, fairness, personal and social responsibility, integrity and self-awareness. Philosophers put forth their views and asserted that the basis of these terms is the function of explicit and implicit values. It is asserted that even if the curriculum may not be intended explicitly, even if the teaching of attitude and values exists in school and makes it possible to manage the conflicts that arise between young students and adults in schools, it is to be noted how young people experience getting involved in their school culture and learning environment. It is the role of the teacher the way the teacher gets the students educated about this concept. It is observed that the process adopted is often implicit; as such, the students do not pay so much attention to this concept, but the teacher must be a feedback practitioner, which keeps the student active in all situations, the teacher must be well aware of his morals and values. So, there is a need to move the process of this course explicitly; this incorporation explicitly and examining values gives the students an opportunity for the modeling of values. It is also observed that morals and values in students are already embedded; it is the skill of the teacher that gets them sparked to get good results, which is by virtue of his quality education.

Education has been viewed since its origin as a way in which students learn to become responsible and moral people. Presently, every country is focusing on the promotion of education, which is a necessity of the day as chaos and hue and cry have come into existence all over the world. This is due to the passion of the materialistic world in the individual and a lack of senses, which has made people self-centered, keeping aside all other relations and benevolence acts. So, to counter this turmoil, education seems to be the only light that can abstain from such ridiculous acts and put the person in the right direction. It helps us in all aspects and can keep our future in a state of well-being. Education brings transparency to the subject so that one has access to criticize, discard, or accept.

Theories of Morality. Morality encompasses guiding principles concerning what is good and bad or what is right and wrong behavior; it enables us to live cooperatively in groups. It introduces us to the concept that everyone has moral values, more or less and in someone one can't define. Philosophers have their theories accordingly; some say it is hereditary that it is a biological product; some say it is the product of humans' interactions with societies; and some say humans hold morality by nature. It is asserted that every creature is a gift to nature, whose prime duty is to save nature and all have senses accordingly. It is also observed that every creature is busy doing some work of its own accord and has its own character, which makes every spice important and proves useful in sustaining the life of nature. Nature can be saved when we all follow the discipline of nature, that is, what is right for nature and this is especially implied on humans as they are the only ones who have the senses of innovation; rest all the creatures live for their survival only, so humans are being held guilty for the deterioration of nature as their actions affect the environment and they get credited by the public accordingly. Morality is such a subtle entity where one's actions always move toward the right, but it is necessary that one must be capable of judging the difference between right and wrong. Darwin, a philosopher whose work on the philosophy of morality asserted that morality is an advanced intelligence that is, equipped in humans to make use of mankind and to keep others aware to follow to sustain the life of nature. They urged that morality is a biological trait but its norms are the collective experience of humans. The philosopher urged that the moral sense is an outcome of intelligentsia, which is only possessed by the human being, which is a natural selection; therefore, we can also consider morality as an outcome of natural selection and further added that it is the human being who sometimes predisposes the events to make moral judgment, which creates doubt in assessing the good and evil. It is also observed that moral codes vary from culture to culture; it does not mean that the sanctity of morality gets affected, but it remains intact as it is, as such, not to harm anybody, honesty is the best policy, etc. God created us with a capacity to know Him and love Him, but it is humans who have a desire to act behaviorally to all in all aspects. Behavior is such an exercise where we may have our identification as it is very much associated with advanced intelligence. So, in every action, one's created norms that proved to be useful and favorable to all beings, with the interest that they may help to sustain the life of nature. This is considered the biggest noble cause maintained by humans, which we call "morality." Therefore, morality is biological and an attribute of advanced intelligence that is, equipped in humans only and nowhere else.

www.ingramcontent.com/pod-product-compliance
Lightning Source LLC
LaVergne TN
LVHW041210150826
845673LV00001B/341

* 9 7 9 8 8 9 1 3 3 4 2 8 1 *